KEN HOM'S
VEGETARIAN
COOKERY

D1143780

KEN HOM'S VEGETARIAN COOKERY

PHOTOGRAPHS BY

GRAHAM KIRK

BBC BOOKS

All food photography: Graham Kirk
Home economist: Allyson Birch
Stylist: Helen Payne

Published by BBC Books,
A division of BBC Enterprises Ltd,
Woodlands, 80 Wood Lane,
London W12 0TT

First published as *Ken Hom's Vegetable & Pasta Book*, 1987
This revised and updated edition first published in 1995

ISBN 0 563 36958 2

Typeset in Sabon by Ace Filmsetting Ltd, Frome, Somerset
Printed and bound in Great Britain by
Richard Clays Ltd, St Ives plc
Colour printed by Lawrence Allen Ltd, Weston-super-Mare

· CONTENTS ·

· ACKNOWLEDGEMENTS ·

A cookery book requires meticulous attention to detail and it is almost impossible for the author, without the help of others, to do everything that must be done to make it as useful and interesting as possible. This book is no exception. I owe an immense debt to Gordon Wing, who is a great chef in his own right. His unerring good taste and expert working and testing of the recipes helped ensure their accuracy. I am grateful to Mimi Luebbermann for her considerable editorial skills and talents of organization. Her vast experience and many useful suggestions helped make this a better book. My thanks and appreciation go to Gerry Cavanaugh, whose skilful research and editing helped me to clarify my thoughts and to present them precisely.

I feel fortunate to be associated with BBC Books and to have Heather Holden-Brown and Julian Flanders as my editors there. I am grateful to them for their generous encouragement.

Credit should go also to Grahame Dudley for the design of the book and to Graham Kirk for the photography.

And for playing no small part in this book and all of my professional activities, my thanks to Carole Blake and Julian Friedmann, my literary agents. Their sound advice and good sense have been of incalculable benefit to me over the years and they have my deep appreciation.

INTRODUCTION

One of the most exciting culinary developments in recent years has been the introduction into Western cuisine of a whole range of Chinese, Japanese and Southeast Asian methods and ingredients, especially the seasonings. Flavours that used to be 'exotic' – chilli oil, coconut milk, lemon grass, bean thread (transparent) noodles, rice wine, star anise, Sichuan peppercorns, soy sauce, fresh ginger and fresh coriander – are now well on their way to becoming standards in home cooking. Most of the recipes in this book are drawn from the Chinese tradition, which is the basis of my own style, and much of the information given in the introductory sections will be familiar to readers of my earlier book on Chinese cookery. However, here I have also included a representative sampling of dishes from other Eastern cuisines.

Each recipe reflects my own tastes and preferences and is drawn from my own observations and experiences – on my travels in Southeast Asia, in restaurants and conversations with other chefs, in my reading and in my culinary experiments. The result is a very personal, eclectic collection which nevertheless has a unified theme: good vegetarian food that is delicious, flavourful and easily prepared, with an oriental flair that blends congenially with a Western meal.

Growing up within the Chinese culinary tradition, fresh vegetables, noodles and pasta – wonderful foods – have been central to my diet in both my personal and professional life ever since I can remember. I use the Italian word 'pasta' because it has entered our vocabulary – covering various forms of unleavened dough, extruded, rolled out, sliced and moulded into different forms. When I was a child, Chinese pasta (of which there are many types, shapes and sizes) and vegetables were as much a part of my diet as were rice and beancurd. As a professional chef, food writer and cookery author, I have always emphasized the role of vegetables and pasta in any cookery. This is especially true as I have become more and more aware of the variety of pastas outside my Chinese influence.

When I became old enough to venture out into the mainstream of Western culture, I was appalled by the way vegetables and pasta were cooked. I had always loved vegetables but I understood my schoolmates' aversion to them, overcooked as they were to the point of limpness and tastelessness. As for pasta, it was gummy and devoid of its customary textures and subtle tastes, overcooked and drowned in tomato sauce. I thought it all quite unnecessary.

In the Chinese cultural environment, food is a source of happiness for both body and soul; meal times are times of an almost religious sharing, of conversation and family interaction, with proper attention having been paid to the preparation of the foods. My mother prepared meat, fish and poultry dishes, but they never dominated our table. Rather, vegetables and pasta, with rice too of course, were the mainstay of our diet. Vegetables, both Chinese and European varieties, were more important to us than meats. And I relished them, finding them flavourful, colourful and cooked to perfection. This means, among other things, that vegetables were preferably as fresh as possible and never overcooked – preserving their natural flavours and nutrients. So too were our noodle and pasta dishes, prepared so that they retained their textures and tastes and were never over-whelmed by any sauce. Pasta, usually in the form of noodles, was enjoyed either as a snack or quick meal, or as an integral part of the complete meal. I savoured them in many forms: fresh or dried egg noodles, flour noodles, rice noodles, wuntuns and spring rolls. Today, of course, I include in my everyday diet the wonderful varieties of European pasta, combined with a blending of oriental seasonings, spices and stuffings.

I agree with a food critic who wrote that the phrase 'al dente' is both overworked and vague; the only workable test of doneness for both vegetables and pasta is the 'nibble test'. Be prepared to nibble or taste your foods during preparation, as only you can tell when they are ready.

I am not a vegetarian myself; my own diet consists primarily of vegetables, rice, pasta or noodles and seafood, with poultry and meat quite secondary and always in small portions. Many of the recipes in this book can accompany other dishes, oriental or not, vegetarian or not, for lunch, dinner or supper. As such, the recipes embody the ideas, tastes, flavours, colours, aromas and aesthetics inspired by my own dual Asian–Western tradition. The recipes are basically authentic but reflect my own tastes and experiences; use them and experiment to make them your own. I can only be a guide on your first steps into this delightful terrain. Your taste and imagination, with loving care in your preparations, will take you much further than any guide could ever do. Happy cooking and eating!

All these are approximate conversions, which have been either rounded up or down. In a few recipes it has been necessary to modify them very slightly. Never mix metric and imperial measures in one recipe. Stick to one system or the other.

WEIGHTS		VOLUME		MEASUREMENTS	
15 g	½ oz	25 ml	1 fl oz	5 mm	¼ in
25	1	50	2	1 cm	½
40	1½	85	3	2.5	1
50	2	150	5 (¼ pint)	5	2
75	3	225	8 (fl oz)	7.5	3
100	4	300	10 (½)	10	4
150	5	400	14	15	6
175	6	450	15 (¾)	18	7
200	7	600	1 pint	20	8
225	8	750	1¼	23	9
250	9	900	1½	25	10
275	10	1 litre	1¾	28	11
350	12	1.2	2	30	12
375	13	1.25	2¼		
400	14	1.5	2½		
425	15	1.6	2¾		

OVEN TEMPERATURES		
140°C	275°F	Gas 1
150	300	2
160	325	3
180	350	4
190	375	5
200	400	6
220	425	7
230	450	8
240	475	9

Remaining WEIGHTS and VOLUME rows:

WEIGHTS		VOLUME	
450	1 lb	1.75	3
550	1¼	2	3½
750	1½	2.25	4
900	2	2.75	5
1.4 kg	3	3.4	6
1.75	4	3.9	7
2.25	5	4.5	8 (1 gal)

· I N G R E D I E N T S ·

Fresh vegetables are, of course, essential to good vegetarian cooking. But equally important are the other ingredients – the seasonings, spices and sauces that complement and enhance the virtues of the vegetables. The recipes in this book draw upon a number of special ingredients which give a distinctive taste to the food, making them authentic versions of the Chinese, Japanese and Southeast Asian originals.

All the ingredients used in these recipes can be obtained in Britain, if not from your local supermarket then certainly from either a Chinese, oriental or Asian grocer. There are now many of these grocers throughout the UK. It is well worth the effort to find your nearest oriental, Chinese or Asian grocer and to build up a stock of the most frequently used ingredients.

One ingredient commonly used, which you will *not* find mentioned here, is the additive monosodium glutamate (also known as MSG, Ve Tsin, Accent, seasoning or taste powder). This is a white crystalline extract of grains and vegetables widely used to tenderize and enhance the natural flavour of certain foods. Some people experience an adverse reaction to it, suffering symptoms such as headaches, excessive thirst and heart palpitations. This allergic response is sometimes known as 'Chinese restaurant syndrome'. I believe that the freshest and finest ingredients need no enhancing and therefore I never use monosodium glutamate.

Below I have listed, in alphabetical order, all the special ingredients used in the book. More detailed information on specific vegetables and types of pasta and noodles is given in the introductions to those chapters.

BAMBOO SHOOTS

Bamboo shoots are the young edible shoots of certain kinds of bamboo. In Britain, they are only available tinned. Pale yellow with a crunchy texture, they come peeled and either whole or thickly sliced.

They can be bought in most supermarkets, delicatessens and in Chinese grocers. Rinse them thoroughly before use and transfer any remaining shoots to a jar, cover them with fresh water and keep in the fridge. If the water is changed daily they will keep for up to a week.

BEANCURD

Beancurd is also known by its Chinese name, 'doufu', or by its Japanese name, 'tofu'. It has played an important part in Chinese cookery for over 1000 years: it is highly nutritious, being rich in protein, and combines well with other foods. Beancurd has a distinctive texture but a bland taste. It is made from yellow soya beans which are soaked, ground, mixed with water and then cooked briefly before being solidified. In Britain, it is usually sold in two forms, firm cakes or as a thickish junket, but it is also available in several dried forms and fermented. The soft junket-like variety (sometimes called silken tofu) is used for soups and other dishes, while the solid type is used for stir-frying, braising and poaching. Solid beancurd 'cakes' are white in colour and are sold in Chinese grocers and in many health food shops. They are packed in water in plastic containers and may be kept in this state in the fridge for up to 5 days, providing the water is changed daily. To use solid beancurd, cut the amount required into cubes or shreds using a sharp knife. Do this with care as it is delicate. Beancurd also needs to be cooked carefully as too much stirring can cause it to disintegrate.

Fermented beancurd

This is a cheese-like form of beancurd preserved in rice wine, brine with rice or chillies, and sold in glass jars in Chinese grocers. It is used as a flavouring agent, especially for vegetables. A little can add zest to any vegetable dish. Once it begins to cook, it produces a fragrant odour that enriches vegetables. Fermented beancurd comes in several forms: the red fermented beancurd has been cured in a brine with red rice, the chilli one has flecks of crushed chilli peppers and the ordinary one is left plain. Once the jar is opened, it should be stored in the fridge, keeping well for several months. There is no substitute for this unique ingredient.

Pressed seasoned beancurd

When water is extracted from fresh beancurd cakes by pressing them with a weight, the beancurd becomes firm and compact. Simmered in water with soy sauce, star anise and sugar, the pressed beancurd acquires a brownish colour and smooth, resilient texture. Cut into small pieces, it can be stir-fried with vegetables; and when cut into larger pieces, it can be simmered. In China, pressed beancurd is a popular offering at many food stalls. It can be found in Chinese grocers. Substitute fresh firm beancurd if it is unavailable.

BLACK BEANS

These small black soya beans, also known as salted black beans, are preserved by being fermented with salt and spices. They have a distinctive, slightly salty taste and a pleasantly rich smell, and are used as a seasoning, often in conjunction with garlic and fresh ginger. Black beans are inexpensive and can be obtained from Chinese grocers, usually in tins, as 'black beans in salted sauce'; you may also see them packed in plastic bags, which are preferable. Rinse before use; I prefer to chop the beans slightly, too. Transfer any unused beans and liquid to a sealed jar and they will keep indefinitely if stored in the fridge.

CHILLIES

Chillies are used extensively in western China and somewhat less frequently in the south, as well as many parts of Southeast Asia. They are the seed pods of the capsicum plant and can be obtained fresh, dried or ground.

Fresh chillies

Fresh chillies can be distinguished by their small size and elongated shape. They should look fresh and bright with no brown patches or black spots. There are several varieties. Red chillies are generally milder than green ones because they sweeten as they ripen.

To prepare fresh chillies, first rinse them in cold water. Using a small sharp knife, slit them lengthways and remove and discard the seeds. Rinse the chillies well under cold running water, and then prepare them according to the instructions in the recipe. Wash your hands, knife and chopping board before preparing other foods, and be careful not to touch your eyes until you have washed your hands thoroughly with soap and water.

Dried red chillies

Dried red chillies are small and thin, and about 1 cm (½ in) long. They are used to season oil for stir-fried dishes, sauces and for braising. Dried chillies are normally left whole or cut in half lengthways and the seeds left in. The Chinese like them to blacken and remain in the dish during cooking, but as they are extremely hot and spicy, you may choose to remove them after using them to flavour the cooking oil. Dried chillies can be found in most supermarkets and in Chinese and oriental grocers, and will keep indefinitely in a tightly covered jar.

Chilli powder

Chilli powder, also known as cayenne pepper, is made from ground dried red chillies. It is pungent, aromatic and ranges from hot to very hot; it is therefore widely used in many spicy dishes. You will be able to buy chilli powder in any supermarket.

Chilli bean sauce (see SAUCES AND PASTES)

Chilli oil (see OILS)

Chilli sauce (see SAUCES AND PASTES)

CINNAMON STICKS/BARK

Cinnamon sticks are curled, paper-thin pieces of the bark of the cinnamon tree. Chinese cinnamon comes as thicker sticks of this bark. It is highly aromatic and more pungent than the more common cinnamon sticks, but the latter are an adequate substitute. They add a robust taste to braised dishes and are an important ingredient of five spice powder. Store cinnamon sticks or bark in a tightly sealed jar to preserve their aroma and flavour. Ground cinnamon is not a satisfactory substitute.

COCONUT MILK

You can make your own coconut milk according to this recipe:

1 small coconut
750 ml (1¼ pints) low-fat milk

6 tablespoons sugar

Pre-heat the oven to 180°C/350°F/Gas 4. To prepare the coconut, pierce two of the 'eyes' in the shell and drain and discard the liquid inside. Place the drained coconut in the oven for about 20 minutes. If this does not crack the shell, split by tapping with a hammer along its line of cleavage. (Wrap the coconut in a towel while cracking it to prevent the small pieces from flying about.) Remove the white meat with a knife, discarding any of the brown skin.

Cut the coconut into small pieces and place in a medium-sized saucepan. Cover with 450 ml (15 fl oz) of the milk and simmer for 10 minutes. Allow to cool, then process in a blender on high speed for 1 minute. Let the coconut stand for 15 minutes, then strain into a bowl. Using the back of a wooden spoon, squeeze all the liquid from the chopped coconut. Return the coconut milk to the pan, add the sugar and remaining milk. Simmer for 5 minutes until the milk thickens. Allow to cool, then chill.

Alternatively you can use the tinned variety. I have found it quite acceptable and a lot less work. Look for the ones from Thailand or Malaysia. You can find them in supermarkets or Chinese or oriental grocers, usually in 400 ml (14 fl oz) or 450 ml (15 fl oz) tins. Shake the tins well before opening to use. If you are using tinned milk, any remainder can be kept in the fridge for at least a week out of the tin.

CORIANDER (CHINESE PARSLEY)

Fresh coriander is one of the relatively few herbs used in Chinese cookery. It looks like flatleaf parsley but its pungent, musky, citrus-like flavour gives it a distinctive and unmistakeable character. Its feathery leaves are often used as a garnish or it can be chopped and then mixed into sauces and stuffings. Parsley may be used as a substitute but, for an authentic Chinese flavour, it is well worth trying to obtain the real thing. Many Chinese, oriental and Asian grocers stock fresh coriander, as do some greengrocers and supermarkets. When buying fresh coriander, look for deep green, fresh-looking leaves. Yellow and limp leaves indicate age and should be avoided.

To store coriander, wash in cold water, drain thoroughly and put it in a clean polythene bag with a couple of sheets of moist kitchen paper. Stored in the vegetable compartment of the fridge, it should keep for several days.

CORNFLOUR

In China and Southeast Asia there are many flours and types of starch, such as waterchestnut powder, taro starch and arrowroot, which are used to bind and thicken sauces and to make batter. These exotic starches and flours are difficult to obtain but I have found cornflour works just as well in my recipes. As part of a marinade, it helps to coat the food properly and gives dishes a velvety texture. Cornflour also protects food during deep-frying by helping to seal in the juices, and it can also be used as a binder for minced stuffings. Cornflour is invariably blended with cold water until it forms a smooth paste before it is used in sauces.

FIVE SPICE POWDER

Five spice powder is less commonly known as five-flavoured powder or five fragrance spice powder, and is available in many supermarkets (in the spice section) and in Chinese grocers. This brownish powder is a mixture of star anise, Sichuan peppercorns, fennel, cloves and cinnamon. A good blend is pungent, fragrant, spicy and slightly sweet at the same time. The exotic fragrance it gives to a dish makes the search for a good mixture well worth the effort. It keeps indefinitely in a well sealed jar.

FLOURS

Glutinous rice flour

This flour is made from glutinous rice and is often used in making pastries to give the chewy texture to the doughs. Available from Chinese grocers, this is not an acceptable substitute for rice flour.

Rice flour

This flour is made from raw rice and is used to make fresh rice noodles. Obtainable from Chinese grocers, it is stored as plain flour.

FUNGUS (*see* MUSHROOMS, CHINESE DRIED)

GARLIC

Garlic has been an essential seasoning in oriental cookery for thousands of years. It would be inconceivable to cook without the distinctive, highly aromatic smell and taste of garlic. Throughout Asia it is used in numerous ways: whole, finely chopped, crushed and pickled. It is used to flavour oils as well as spicy sauces, and is often paired with other equally pungent ingredients such as spring onions, black beans, curry or fresh ginger.

Select fresh garlic which is firm and preferably pinkish in colour. It should be stored in a cool, dry place but not in the fridge where it can easily become mildewed or begin sprouting.

GINGER

Fresh root ginger (actually a rhizome, not a root) is indispensable in oriental cookery. Its pungent, spicy and fresh taste adds a subtle but distinctive flavour to soups, sauces and vegetables. Fresh ginger looks rather like a gnarled Jerusalem artichoke and can range in size from 7.5 cm (3 in) to 15 cm (6 in) long. It has pale brown, dry skin which is usually peeled away before use. Select fresh ginger which is firm with no signs of shrivelling. It will keep in the fridge, well wrapped in cling film, for up to 2 weeks. Fresh ginger can now be found at many greengrocers and supermarkets, and in most Chinese and oriental grocers. Dried powdered ginger has a quite different flavour and cannot be substituted for fresh ginger.

Ginger juice

Ginger juice is made from fresh ginger and is used in cooking to give a subtle ginger taste without the bite of the chopped fresh pieces. To make ginger juice, simply take a piece of fresh ginger and smash it with a kitchen mallet or the side of a cleaver or knife until most of the fibres are exposed. Then, with a garlic press or your hands, simply squeeze out the juice. The left-over ginger can be used to flavour the oil before you cook. The fresh ginger juice must be used immediately.

LEMON GRASS

This aromatic lemony tropical grass is widely used in Southeast Asian cooking and is found in Chinese and oriental grocers. Look for pale green tops and make sure the lemon grass is not dried out. Cut off the fibrous base and peel away the outside layers. Cut off the tops and save to flavour oils or soups. Lemon juice or lemon zest can be used as a substitute. Lemon grass can be sliced and frozen for future use.

LILY BUDS

Also known as tiger lily buds, golden needles or lily stems, dried lily buds (*Lilium lancifolium*) are an ingredient in Mu-Shu dishes and hot and sour soups. They add more texture than taste. Soak the buds in hot water for about 30 minutes or until soft. Cut off the hard ends and shred or cut in half according to the recipe.

MUSHROOMS, CHINESE DRIED

There are many varieties of these which add a particular flavour and aroma to Chinese dishes. These mushrooms can be black or brown in colour. The very large ones, with a lighter colour and a highly cracked surface, are the best and so they are usually the most expensive. They can be bought in boxes or plastic bags from Chinese grocers, and are fairly pricey. Keep them stored in an airtight jar in a cool dry place.

To use Chinese dried mushrooms

Soak the required amount in hot water for about 20 minutes until soft. Squeeze out any excess liquid and remove the tough, inedible stalk. The mushrooms are now ready for use. The resulting liquid can be used for cooking rice – simply pour off the liquid gently, leaving any sand or residue behind.

Chinese dried cloud ears (black fungus)

These tiny dried mushrooms are known as cloud ears because when soaked, they look like little clouds. Soak the cloud ears in hot water for 20–30 minutes until soft. Rinse well and cut away any hard pieces. They are valued for their crunchy texture and slightly smokey flavour. There is some medical research that indicates they are of value in the prevention of heart disease. You can find cloud ears in Chinese or oriental grocers, usually wrapped in plastic or cellophane bags. They keep indefinitely in a jar stored in a cool dry place.

Chinese dried wood ears

These mushrooms are the larger variety of cloud ears. Prepare and soak them in the same way, then rinse well. Once soaked, they will swell up to four or five times their size. Cut away any hard pieces. Sold in Chinese or oriental grocers, they keep indefinitely when stored in a cool dry place.

Nori (*see* Seaweed)

Oils

Oil is the most commonly used cooking medium in China, Japan and Southeast Asia. The favourite is groundnut (peanut) oil.

I find oils are best re-used just once or twice; this is healthier since constantly re-using oils increases the saturated fat content. To prepare oil for re-use, simply cool the oil after use and filter it through muslin or a fine strainer into a jar. Cover tightly and keep in a cool, dry place. If you keep oil in the fridge it will become cloudy, but it clarifies again at room temperature.

Groundnut oil

This is also known as peanut oil or arachide oil. I prefer to use this because it has a pleasant, mild taste which is unobtrusive. Although it has a higher saturated fat content than some oils, its ability to be heated to a high temperature makes it perfect for stir-frying and deep-frying. Many supermarkets stock groundnut oil, but if you cannot find it use corn oil instead.

Corn oil

Corn or maize oil is also quite suitable for cooking. It has a high heating point although I find it rather bland, plus it has a slightly disagreeable smell. Corn oil is high in polyunsaturates and is therefore one of the healthier oils.

Other vegetable oils

Some of the cheaper vegetable oils available include soyabean, safflower and sunflower oils. They are light in colour and taste, and can also be used in cooking.

Sesame oil

This is a thick, rich, golden brown oil made from sesame seeds, which has a distinctive, nutty flavour and aroma. It is widely used in Chinese and Japanese cookery as a seasoning, but is not normally used as a cooking oil because it heats rapidly and burns easily. It is often added at the last moment to finish a dish. It is sold in bottles in many supermarkets and in Chinese or oriental grocers.

Chilli oil

Chilli oil is an essential ingredient in many of the recipes in this book.

This is to be expected, inasmuch as it is a staple condiment/flavouring throughout Asia. You may purchase it in Chinese, oriental or Asian grocers and specialist food shops. The Thai and Malaysian versions are especially hot; the Hong Kong, Taiwanese and Chinese versions are a little milder. Such commercial products are quite acceptable and I include this recipe only because the home-made version is the best. Remember that chilli oil is too dramatic to be used directly in cooking; it is best applied as a final spicy touch. I include the spices (pepper and black beans) for additional flavours, because then it can also be used as a dipping sauce. If you prefer a milder taste, you can reduce the quantity of chopped dried chillies.

Once made, the chilli oil can be put in a tightly sealed glass jar and stored in a cool dark place where it will keep for months.

Chilli Oil/Dipping Sauce

150 ml (5 fl oz) oil, preferably groundnut	1 tablespoon unroasted whole Sichuan peppercorns
2 tablespoons chopped dried red chillies	2 tablespoons whole black beans

Heat a frying-pan or wok over a high heat and add the oil. Put in the rest of the ingredients and cook over a low heat for about 10 minutes. Allow the mixture to cool undisturbed and then pour it into a jar. Leave the mixture to stand for 2 days. Strain and discard the solids from the chilli oil, returning the oil to the glass jar for use in recipes. It will keep indefinitely.

PEANUTS

Raw peanuts are used in oriental cooking to add flavour and a crunchy texture, and are especially popular in Southeast Asian cooking. They can be bought in health food shops, good supermarkets and Chinese grocers. The thin red skins need to be removed before you use the nuts. To do this, simply immerse them in a pan of boiling water for about 2 minutes. Drain them, leave to cool and the skins will come off easily.

RED-IN-SNOW

This is Chinese pickled cabbage that can be bought in tins in Chinese grocers. It adds a pungent, slightly sour taste to dishes when used as a flavouring, or it can be used as an interestingly textured vegetable in stir-fried dishes.

RICE WINE

This wine is used extensively for cooking and drinking throughout China and the finest variety is believed to be that from Shaoxing in Zhejiang Province in eastern China. It is made from glutinous rice, yeast and spring water. Available from Chinese grocers, it should be kept at room temperature, tightly corked. A good quality, dry pale sherry can be substituted but cannot equal the rich, mellow taste of Chinese rice wine. Do not confuse this with sake, which is the Japanese version of rice wine and quite different.

SAKE

Sake is a Japanese rice wine often used in Japanese cooking. It should not be confused with Mirin which is a much sweeter wine and cannot be used as a substitute. The more expensive brands are served gently warmed as a drink, but less expensive brands are suitable for cooking. If you do not like the alcohol taste, briefly bring the sake to the boil before combining with other ingredients.

SAUCES AND PASTES

Chinese, Japanese and Southeast Asian cookery all involve thick, tasty sauces or pastes. They are essential to the authentic taste of the food. Most are sold in bottles or tins in Chinese or oriental grocers and some supermarkets. Tinned sauces, once opened, should be transferred to screw-top glass jars and kept in the fridge, where they will last for a long time.

Chilli bean sauce

This is a thick dark sauce or paste made from soya beans, chillies and other seasonings, and is very hot and spicy. Widely used in cooking in western China, it is usually available in Britain in jars in Chinese grocers. Be sure to seal the jar tightly after use and store in the larder or fridge. Do not confuse it with chilli sauce (see over) which is a hot, red, thinner sauce made without beans and used mainly as a dipping sauce for cooked dishes. There are Southeast Asian versions of chilli bean sauce and I find them very spicy and hot. You can use these if you like, but throughout this book, I have used the Chinese chilli bean sauce which is slightly milder.

Chilli sauce

Chilli sauce is a hot, bright red sauce made from chillies, vinegar, sugar and salt. It is sometimes used for cooking, but mainly as a dipping sauce. There are various brands available in many supermarkets and Chinese grocers and you should experiment with them until you find the one you like best. If you find it too strong, dilute with hot water. Do not confuse this sauce with the chilli bean sauce mentioned previously, which is a much thicker, darker sauce used for cooking.

Curry paste

This prepared paste has a stronger curry flavour than the powdered variety. The spices are mixed with oil and chilli peppers. Be sure to get the Indian variety which is generally the best. You can find curry paste in Asian or Chinese grocers. Kept chilled after opening, curry paste keeps indefinitely.

Dipping sauces and mixtures

Many Chinese and Southeast Asian dishes and snacks are dipped into a variety of dipping sauces before being eaten. The most popular of these are chilli sauce and chilli oil (see Oils). Soy sauces and red and black Chinese rice vinegars (see Vinegars) are also widely used as dips. Some recipes for dipping sauces accompany particular dishes, but they can easily be served with others.

Hoisin sauce

This is a thick, dark, brownish red sauce, made from soya beans, vinegar, sugar, spices and other flavourings. It is sweet and spicy and is widely used in southern Chinese cookery. In the West, it is often used as a sauce for Peking Duck instead of the traditional sweet bean sauce. Hoisin sauce, sometimes called barbecue sauce, is sold in tins and jars, and is available in Chinese grocers and some supermarkets. If chilled, it should keep indefinitely.

Sesame paste

This rich, thick, creamy brown paste is made from sesame seeds. It is used in both hot and cold dishes, and is particularly popular in northern and western China. Sesame paste is sold in jars in Chinese grocers. If you cannot obtain it, use peanut butter.

SOY SAUCES

Soy sauce is an essential ingredient in Chinese and Southeast Asian cooking. It is made from a mixture of soya beans, flour and water, which is then naturally fermented and matured for some months. The liquid which is finally distilled is soy sauce. There are two main types, light and dark.

Light soy sauce

As the name implies, this is light in colour but it is full of flavour and is the best one to use for cooking. It is saltier than dark soy sauce. In Chinese grocers, light soy sauce is known as Superior Soy. If you are preparing standard Chinese recipes using fish sauce, you can substitute light soy sauce.

Dark soy sauce

This sauce is matured for much longer than light soy sauce, hence its darker, almost black, colour. Slightly thicker and stronger than light soy sauce, it is more suitable for stews. I prefer it to light soy sauce as a dipping sauce. It is known in Chinese grocers as Soy Superior Sauce. If you use standard Chinese recipes using oyster sauce, you can substitute dark soy sauce.

Most soy sauces sold in supermarkets are dark soy. Chinese grocers sell both types and the quality is superior. Be sure you buy the right one as the names are very similar.

Yellow bean sauce

This thick, spicy, aromatic sauce is made with yellow beans, flour and salt which are fermented together. It is quite salty but adds a distinctive flavour to Chinese sauces. There are two forms: whole beans in a thick sauce or mashed or puréed beans (sold as crushed yellow bean sauce). I prefer the whole bean variety because it is slightly less salty and has a better texture. It keeps best in the fridge.

SEAWEED

Known as nori, seaweed is a nutritious and ancient food. Often used in soups and as a wrapper for sushi, it has a delicate flavour. Nori comes packaged in ten or more thinly pressed dried sheets. Individual recipes use different techniques for soaking and cooking seaweed.

SESAME SEEDS

These are dried seeds of an oriental annual herb. Unhulled, the seeds range from greyish white to black in colour, but once the hull is removed, the sesame seeds are flat, tiny, creamy coloured, and pointed at one end. Sesame seeds are valued as a flavouring agent and as a source of oil and paste. Sesame seeds can be found in supermarkets or Chinese grocers. Kept in a glass jar in a cool dry place, they will last indefinitely.

To toast sesame seeds

Pre-heat the oven to 160°C/325°F/Gas 3. Spread the sesame seeds on a baking tray. Roast in the oven for about 10–15 minutes until they are lightly browned. Allow the toasted seeds to cool, then store them in a glass jar.

SHERRY

If you cannot obtain rice wine, you can use a good quality, dry, pale sherry instead. Do not use sweet or cream sherries.

SICHUAN PEPPERCORNS

Sichuan peppercorns are known throughout China as 'flower peppers' because they look like flower buds opening. They are reddish brown in colour with a strong pungent odour, which distinguishes them from the hotter black peppercorns. Sichuan peppercorns are not from peppers at all, but are the dried berries of a shrub which is a member of the citrus family. I find their smell reminds me of lavender, while their taste is sharp and mildly spicy. They can be ground in a conventional peppermill and are very often roasted before grinding to bring out their full flavour. Sold wrapped in cellophane or plastic bags in Chinese grocers, Sichuan peppercorns are inexpensive. They will keep indefinitely if stored in a well sealed container.

To roast Sichuan peppercorns

Heat a wok or heavy frying-pan to medium heat. Add the peppercorns (you can cook up to about 150 g [5 oz] at a time) and stir-fry for about 5 minutes until they brown slightly and start to smoke. Remove the pan from the heat and leave to cool. Grind the peppercorns in a peppermill, clean coffee grinder or with a pestle and mortar. Seal the mixture tightly in a screw-top jar to store. Alternatively, keep the whole roasted peppercorns in a well sealed container and grind them when required.

SICHUAN PRESERVED VEGETABLE

There are many types of Chinese pickled vegetables. One of the most popular is Sichuan preserved vegetable, a speciality of Sichuan Province. This is the root of the mustard green which is pickled in salt and hot chillies. Another type is Sichuan preserved cabbage. Sold in tins in Chinese grocers, they give a pleasantly crunchy texture and spicy taste to dishes. Before using the preserved vegetable, rinse in cold water and then slice or chop as required. Any unused vegetable should be transferred to a tightly covered jar and stored in the fridge where the preserved vegetable should keep indefinitely. If you use ordinary Chinese recipes using dried shrimps, you can substitute preserved vegetables.

STAR ANISE

The star anise is a hard, star-shaped spice and is the seed-pod of the anise bush. (It is also known as Chinese anise or whole anise.) It is similar in flavour and fragrance to common aniseed but is more robust and liquorice-like. Star anise is an essential ingredient of five spice powder and is widely used in braised dishes to which it imparts a rich taste and fragrance. Sold in plastic packs in Chinese grocers or supermarkets, star anise should be stored in a tightly covered jar in a cool, dry place.

SUGAR

Sugar has been used in the cooking of savoury dishes in China for a thousand years. Properly employed, it helps balance the various flavours of sauces and other dishes. Chinese sugar comes in several forms: rock or yellow lump sugar, brown sugar slabs and as maltose or malt sugar. I particularly like to use rock sugar, which is rich and has a more subtle flavour than refined granulated sugar. It also gives a good lustre or glaze to braised dishes and sauces. You can buy this in Chinese grocers. You may need to break the lumps into smaller pieces with a wooden mallet or rolling pin. If you cannot find this, use white sugar or coffee sugar crystals (the amber, chunky kind) instead.

VINEGARS

Vinegars are widely used in Chinese, Southeast Asian and Japanese cooking. Unlike Western vinegars, they are usually made from rice. There are many varieties, ranging in flavour from the spicy and slightly tart to the sweet and pungent, and all can be bought from Chinese grocers. They are sold in bottles and will keep indefinitely. If you cannot obtain Chinese vinegars, I suggest you use cider vinegar instead. Malt vinegar can be used, but its taste is stronger and more acidic.

Black rice vinegar

Black rice vinegar is very dark in colour and rich though mild in taste. It is used for braised dishes, noodles and sauces.

Red rice vinegar

Red rice vinegar is sweet and spicy in taste and is usually used as a dipping sauce for seafood.

White rice vinegar

White rice vinegar is clear and mild in flavour. It has a faint taste of glutinous rice and is used for sweet and sour dishes.

WONTON SKINS

Wonton skins are made from egg and flour and can be bought fresh or frozen from Chinese grocers. They are thin pastry-like wrappings which can be stuffed with vegetables or sweet fillings, and fried, steamed or used in soups. They are sold in little piles of 8 cm (3¼ in) yellowish squares, wrapped in plastic. The number of squares or skins in a packet varies from about 30 to 36, depending upon the supplier. Fresh wonton skins will keep for about 5 days if stored in cling film or a plastic bag in the fridge. If you are using frozen wonton skins, just peel off the number you require and thaw thoroughly before you use them.

· E Q U I P M E N T ·

Much of the equipment used in other oriental cookery is similar to the Chinese, so I will discuss traditional Chinese cooking equipment. While not essential for cooking Southeast Asian, Japanese or Chinese food, there are a few pieces of equipment which will make it very much easier. Most items can be bought very cheaply, especially if you seek out authentic implements from a Chinese or oriental grocer, and you can now find fairly good versions sold in many department stores.

WOK

The most useful piece of equipment is the wok, in which it is easier to toss foods quickly without spilling them. It also requires far less oil for deep-frying than a deep-fat fryer, although you may find the latter easier and safer to use. Another advantage is that the shape of the wok allows the heat to spread evenly over its surface, thus making for rapid cooking which is fundamental to stir-frying.

There are two types of wok: the Cantonese wok which has a short, rounded handle on either side, and the pau wok which has one long handle. The Cantonese wok is best for steaming and deep-frying since it can be set steadily onto a stand over the heat, and is easier to move when it is full of liquid. The pau wok is better for stir-frying since it is easier to shake over the heat with one hand while your free hand wields a long-handled spoon or spatula. It also distances you from the heat and hot oil and makes for more comfortable, safer frying. Woks with rounded bases should only be used on gas hobs. It is now possible to buy woks with flattish bottoms which are specifically designed for electric hobs, but can be used with gas as well. Although these really defeat the purpose of the traditional design, which is to concentrate intense heat at the centre, they do have the advantage of having deeper sides than a frying-pan.

Choosing a wok

Choose a large wok – preferably about 30–35 cm (12–14 in) in diameter, with good deep sides. Some woks on the market are too shallow and are no better than a large frying-pan. Clearly, it is easier to cook a small quantity in a large wok than to try to accommodate a large quantity in a small one. Select one which is heavy and, if possible, made of carbon steel rather than a light stainless steel or aluminium. The latter types tend to scorch. Non-stick woks are more expensive, and cannot be seasoned like an ordinary wok. I dislike electric woks because I find they do not heat up to a sufficiently high temperature and tend to be too shallow.

Seasoning a wok

All woks (except non-stick ones) need to be seasoned. Many need to be scrubbed first as well to remove the machine oil which is applied to the surface by the manufacturer to protect it in transit. This is the *only* time you will ever scrub your wok – unless you let it rust up. Scrub it with a cream cleanser and water to remove as much of the machine oil as possible. Then dry it and put it on the hob on a low heat. Add 2 tablespoons of cooking oil and rub this over the inside of the wok using kitchen paper until the entire surface is lightly coated with oil. Heat the wok slowly for about 10–15 minutes and then wipe it thoroughly with more kitchen paper. The paper will become blackened. Repeat this process of coating, heating and wiping until the kitchen paper wipes clean. Your wok will darken and become well seasoned with use.

Cleaning a wok

Do not scrub a seasoned wok. Just wash it in plain water without detergent. Dry it thoroughly, preferably by putting it over a low heat for a few minutes before storing. This should prevent the wok from rusting, but if it does, scrub the rust off with a cream cleanser and repeat the seasoning process.

WOK ACCESSORIES

Wok stand

This is a metal ring or frame designed to keep a conventionally shaped wok steady on the hob, and is essential if you want to use your wok for steaming, deep-frying or braising. Stands come in in two designs. One is a solid metal ring with about six ventilation holes. The other is a circular thin wire frame. If you have a gas cooker, *use only the latter type*, as the more solid design does not allow for sufficient ventilation and may lead to a build-up of gas which could put the flame out completely.

Wok lid

A wok lid is a dome-like cover, usually made from aluminium, which is used for steaming. It may come with the wok or it can be purchased separately from a Chinese grocer, but any large domed pan lid which fits snugly over the top of the wok can be used instead. Alternatively, you could use foil.

Spatula

A long-handled metal spatula shaped rather like a small shovel is ideal for scooping and tossing food in a wok. Any good long-handled spoon can be used instead.

Rack

If you use your wok or a large pan as a steamer you will need a wooden or metal rack or trivet to stand above the water level and support the plate of food to be steamed. Some woks are sold with a metal stand, but most Chinese grocers, department stores and hardware shops stock triangular wooden stands or round metal stands which can be used for this purpose. You can improvise a stand by using an empty, inverted tin can of suitable height.

DEEP-FAT FRYERS

These are very useful, and you may find them safer and easier to use for deep-frying than a wok. *The quantities of oil given in the recipes are based on the amount required for deep-frying in a wok. If you are using a deep-fat fryer instead you will need about double that amount, but never fill it more than half-full with oil.*

CLEAVERS

No self-respecting Chinese or Southeast Asian cook would be seen with a knife instead of a cleaver. These heavy choppers serve many purposes. They are used for all kinds of cutting, ranging from fine shredding to chopping up bones. A Chinese cook would usually have three types: a lightweight one with a narrow blade for cutting delicate foods including vegetables; a medium-weight one for general cutting, chopping and crushing purposes; and a heavy one for heavy-duty chopping. Of course, you can prepare Chinese food using good sharp knives, but if you decide to invest in a cleaver, you will be surprised at how easy it is to use. Choose a good quality stainless steel one and keep it sharp.

CHOPPING BOARD

The Chinese traditionally use a soft wood block for chopping, but these blocks are not only difficult to maintain, they also accumulate bacteria. Therefore, I prefer to use a hardwood or acrylic board. Both are strong, easy to clean and last indefinitely. There is so much chopping and slicing to be done when preparing food for Chinese-style cooking that it really is essential to have a large, steady cutting board. Always clean your cutting boards properly after use. Vinegar or lemon works well.

STEAMERS

Bamboo steamers are among the most ancient of Chinese cooking utensils. These attractive round 'boxes' come in several sizes of which the 25 cm (10 in) size is the most suitable for home use. Bamboo steamers are filled with food and placed on top of a pan or over a wok of boiling water. Clean damp muslin is sometimes placed over the open slats under the food to prevent sticking. A tight-fitting bamboo lid is put on top to prevent the steam escaping. One of the advantages of the design is that several steamers can be stacked on top of the other for multiple cooking. Bamboo steamers can be bought in Chinese grocers. (Alternatively, any European kind of wide, metal steamer can be used.) Before using a bamboo steamer for the first time, wash and steam it empty for about 5 minutes.

RICE COOKERS

Electric rice cookers are increasing in popularity. They cook rice perfectly and keep it warm throughout a meal. A rice cooker also has the advantage of freeing a burner or element, making for a less cluttered hob. They are relatively expensive, however, so unless you eat rice frequently I do not think they are worth the expense.

CHOPSTICKS

Chopsticks are not just used for eating in Chinese and Southeast Asian cooking (with the exception of Thais, who use forks). They are also used when cooking, for stirring, beating and whipping. Special long chopsticks are available for these purposes, but it is perfectly all right to use Western cooking implements instead.

Table chopsticks come in wood, plastic and, most luxurious of all, in silver. They can be bought from many department stores, Chinese grocers and many Chinese restaurants or take-aways.

▪ T E C H N I Q U E S ▪

The preparation of food before cooking is probably more important and more time-consuming in Chinese, Japanese and Southeast Asian cookery than in any other cuisine. However, because the subject of this book is vegetarian cooking, many of the recipes are simpler and easier to make than those dealing with meats and poultry. It is important, nonetheless, to have all ingredients properly prepared beforehand. In stir-frying, for example, the food must be chopped into small, well-shaped pieces. This will ensure even and quick cooking, and is especially important for vegetables so as to avoid overcooking. Foods prepared and cooked this way retain their natural textures and tastes. Another reason for careful cutting is to enhance the visual appeal of a dish. This is why most Chinese and Southeast Asian cuisines are so specific about cutting techniques, particularly where vegetables are concerned. The Chinese always use a cleaver (see p.29) for these tasks, wielding it with skill and dexterity, but a sharp heavy knife can be used instead.

Chinese cookery is a sophisticated cuisine which involves a number of cooking methods which are relatively uncommon in the West; many of them have been adopted in other Southeast Asian cuisines. Sometimes several different cooking techniques are used in the preparation of a single dish, such as deep-frying beancurd and then braising it. Most of these techniques can be easily mastered with a little practice. When you are planning a meal, be sure to select dishes which use a range of techniques; limit yourself to one stir-fried dish per meal until you have become used to this important method of cooking.

CUTTING TECHNIQUES

Slicing
This is the conventional method of slicing food. Hold the food firmly on the chopping board with one hand and slice the food straight down into very thin slices. If you use a cleaver rather than a knife for this, hold the cleaver with your index finger over the far side of the top of

the cleaver and your thumb on the side nearest you to guide the cutting edge firmly. Hold the food with your other hand, turning your fingers under for safety. Your knuckles should act as a guide for the blade.

Horizontal or flat slicing

There is a technique for splitting food into two thinner pieces while retaining its overall shape. It can be used for cutting beancurd in half, for example. The cleaver, with its wide blade, is particularly suitable for this. Hold the blade of the cleaver or knife parallel to the chopping board and place your free hand on top of the piece of food to keep it steady. Using a gentle cutting motion, slice horizontally through the food.

Diagonal slicing

This technique is used for cutting vegetables such as asparagus, carrots or spring onions. The purpose is to expose more of the surface of the vegetable for quicker cooking. Angle the knife or cleaver at a slant and cut.

Roll cutting

This is rather like diagonal slicing but is used for larger vegetables such as courgettes, large carrots, aubergines and Chinese white radish (mooli). As with diagonal slicing, this technique allows more of the surface of the vegetable to be exposed to the heat, thereby speeding up the cooking time. Begin by making one diagonal slice at one end of the vegetable. Then turn it 180 degrees and make the next diagonal slice. Continue in this way until you have chopped the entire vegetable into evenly sized, diamond-shaped chunks.

Shredding

This is the process by which food is cut into thin, fine, matchstick-like shreds. First cut the food into slices, then pile several slices on top of each other and cut them *lengthways* into fine strips.

Dicing

This is a simple technique of cutting food into small cubes or dice. The food should first be cut into slices. Stack the slices and cut them again *lengthways* into sticks just as you would for shredding (above). Stack the strips or sticks and cut *crossways* into evenly sized cubes or dice.

Scoring

This is a technique used to pierce the surface of foods to help them cook faster and more evenly. It also gives them an attractive appearance. Use a cleaver or sharp knife and make cuts into the food at a slight angle to a depth of about 3 mm (⅛ in). Take care not to cut all the way through. Make cuts all over the surface of the food, cutting criss-cross to give a wide, diamond-shaped pattern.

Cooking Techniques

Blanching

This involves putting food into hot water or into moderately hot oil for a few minutes to cook it briefly but not entirely. It is a sort of softening-up process to prepare the food for final cooking. Blanching in water is common with harder vegetables such as broccoli or carrots. The vegetable is plunged into boiling water for several minutes. It is then drained and plunged into cold water to arrest the cooking process. In such cases, blanching usually precedes stir-frying which completes the cooking.

Poaching

This is a method of simmering food until it is partially cooked. It is then put into soup or combined with a sauce and the cooking process continued.

Stir-frying

This is the most famous of all Chinese cooking techniques and is used extensively. It is possibly the most tricky technique since success with it depends upon having all the required ingredients prepared, measured out and immediately to hand, and on having a good source of fierce heat. Its advantage is that, properly executed, stir-fried foods can be cooked in minutes in very little oil so they retain their natural flavours and textures. It is very important that stir-fried foods should not be overcooked or greasy. Once you have mastered this technique you will find that it becomes almost second nature. Using a wok is definitely an advantage when stir-frying as its shape not only conducts the heat well but its high sides enable you to toss and stir ingredients rapidly, keeping them constantly moving while cooking. Having prepared all the ingredients for stir-frying, follow the steps below.

▨ Heat the wok or frying-pan until it is very hot *before* adding the oil. This prevents food sticking and will ensure an even heat. Add the oil and, using a metal spatula or long-handled spoon, distribute it evenly over the surface. It should be very hot indeed – almost smoking – before you add the next ingredient unless you are going on to flavour the oil (see next point).

If you are flavouring the oil with garlic, spring onions, ginger, dried red chilli or other seasoning, do not wait for the oil to get so hot that it is almost smoking. If you do, these ingredients will burn and become bitter. Toss them quickly in the oil for a few seconds. In some recipes these flavourings will then be removed and discarded before cooking proceeds.

Now add the ingredients as described in the recipe and proceed to stir-fry by tossing them over the surface of the wok or pan with the metal spatula or long-handled spoon. Keep moving the food from the centre of the wok to the sides. Stir-frying is a noisy business and is usually accompanied by quite a lot of spluttering because of the high temperature at which the food must be cooked.

Some stir-fried dishes are thickened with a mixture of cornflour and cold water. To avoid getting a lumpy sauce be sure to remove the wok or pan from the heat before you add the cornflour mixture, which must be thoroughly blended before it is added. The sauce can then be returned to the heat and thickened.

Deep-frying

This is one of the most important techniques in Chinese cookery. The trick is to regulate the heat so that the surface of the food is sealed but does not brown so fast that the food is uncooked inside. Although deep-fried food must not be greasy, the process does require a lot of oil. The Chinese use a wok for deep-frying which requires rather less oil than a deep-fat fryer; however, I think you should avoid using a wok until you are very sure of it. When you do, be certain that it is fully secure on its stand before adding the oil or, if it is flat-bottomed, that it is secured on its own. On no account leave the wok un-supervised. Most people will find a deep-fat fryer easier and safer to use. Be careful not to fill this more than half-full with oil. Below are some points to bear in mind when deep-frying.

Wait for the oil to get hot enough before adding the food to be fried. The oil should give off a haze and almost produce little wisps of smoke when it is the right temperature, but you can test it by dropping in a small piece of food. If it bubbles all over then the oil is sufficiently hot. Adjust the heat as necessary to prevent the oil from actually smoking or over-heating.

Be sure to dry food to be deep-fried thoroughly first with kitchen paper as this will prevent spluttering. If the food is in a marinade, remove it with a slotted spoon and drain before putting it into the oil. If you are using batter, make sure all the excess batter drips off before adding the food to the hot oil.

Oil used for deep-frying can be re-used. Cool it and then strain into a jar through several layers of muslin or through a fine mesh to remove any particles of food which might otherwise burn if re-heated and give the oil a bitter taste. Label the jar according to what food you have cooked in the oil, and only re-use it for the same purpose. Oil can be used up to three times before it begins to lose its effectiveness.

Shallow-frying or pan-frying

This technique is similar to sautéeing. It involves more oil than stir-frying but less than for deep-frying. Food is fried first on one side and then on the other. Sometimes the excess oil is drained off and a sauce added to complete the dish. A frying-pan or a flat-bottomed wok is ideal for shallow-frying.

Slow-simmering and steeping

These processes are very similar. In slow-simmering, food is immersed in liquid which is brought almost to the boil and then the temperature is reduced so that it simmers, cooking the food to the desired degree. This is the technique used for making stock. In steeping, food is similarly immersed in liquid (usually stock) and simmered for a time. The heat is then turned off and the residual heat of the liquid finishes off the cooking process.

Braising and red-braising

These techniques are most often applied to certain vegetables. The food is usually browned or deep-fried and then put into stock which has been flavoured with seasonings and spices. The stock is brought to the boil, the heat reduced and the food simmered gently until it is cooked. Red-braising, which is also known as red-cooking, is simply the technique by which food is braised in a dark liquid such as soy sauce. This gives food a reddish brown colour, hence the name. This type of braising sauce can be saved and frozen for re-use. It can be re-used many times and becomes richer in flavour.

Steaming

Steaming has been used by the Chinese for thousands of years. Along with stir-frying and deep-frying, it is the most widely used technique. Steamed foods are cooked by a gentle moist heat which must circulate freely in order to cook the food. It is an excellent method for bringing out subtle flavours. Vegetables are rarely steamed; they are blanched instead. Bamboo steamers are used by the Chinese, but you could choose from a variety of utensils.

Using a bamboo steamer in a wok   For this you need a large bamboo steamer about 25 cm (10 in) wide. Put about 5 cm (2 in) of water in a wok and bring to simmering point. Put the bamboo steamer containing the food into the wok where it should rest safely perched on the sloping sides. Cover the steamer with its matching lid and steam the food until it is cooked. Replenish the water as required.

Using a wok as a steamer   Put about 5 cm (2 in) of water into a wok and then place a metal or wooden rack into the wok. Bring the water to simmering point and put the food to be steamed onto a heatproof plate. Lower the plate onto the rack and cover the wok tightly with the lid. Check the water level from time to time and replenish it with hot water when necessary.

Using a large roasting tin or pan as a steamer   Put a metal or wooden rack into the tin or pan and pour in about 5 cm (2 in) of water. Bring to simmering point and put the food to be steamed onto a heatproof plate. Lower the plate onto the rack and cover the tin or pan with a lid or foil. Replenish the water as necessary.

If you do not have a metal or wooden rack, you could use a small empty tin to support the plate of food. Remember that the food needs to remain above the water level and must not get wet. The water level should always be at least 2.5 cm (1 in) below the edge of the plate. (Be sure to use a heatproof plate.)

Using a European steamer   If you have a metal steamer which is wide enough to take a plate of food then this will give you very satisfactory results. Keep an eye on the level of the water in the base.

Re-heating foods

Steaming is one of the best methods of re-heating food since it warms the food without cooking it further and without drying it out. To re-heat soups and braised dishes, bring the liquid slowly to a simmer but do not boil. Remove it from the heat as soon as it is hot to prevent overcooking.

CHAPTER ONE

STARTERS AND APPETIZERS

Starters or appetizers are meant to stimulate the palate, to prepare one for the offerings to come. As such, I like them to be subtly appealing in taste and textures. In most cases they should be simple and light, for you don't wish to overwhelm the main course. And yet some appetizers, like Northern Chinese Vegetable Potstickers, are almost a meal in themselves. Indeed, it is not uncommon when dining out in a Chinese restaurant to see people make their selections only from the starters section of the menu. The rule here is to make and use the recipes as they fit into your meal or menu. They may be used as starters; as a first course in a series of courses; or as a part of many courses – that is, if you wish to follow the Chinese custom of including different courses on the table at once; or you may serve them as another dish in a family meal. Use these starters with all styles of cookery, not just Chinese. Be imaginative – combine or match these appetizers with other foods and beverages, or serve them as mini meals in themselves.

· THAI SWEETCORN PANCAKES ·
Serves 4–6

Sweetcorn is one of the numerous 'New World' vegetables – along with tomatoes, white and sweet potatoes, peppers, chillies – introduced relatively recently into China and Southeast Asia and now extremely popular ingredients in these cuisines. Thai cookery often uses sweetcorn in its dishes and these hot and spicy pancakes are typical of Thai food. I prefer it even hotter, but if you wish you may cut down on the chillies. Delicious served warm or cold, these pancakes make an excellent starter but may also be served as a side vegetable dish to a main course.

900 g (2 lb) fresh sweetcorn on the cob, or 550 g (1¼ lb) tinned sweetcorn
2 eggs, beaten
1 tablespoon cornflour
2 tablespoons chopped fresh coriander
1 tablespoon finely chopped garlic
2 tablespoons finely chopped fresh ginger
¼ teaspoon black pepper
1 teaspoon salt
2 tablespoons coarsely chopped fresh chillies
1 tablespoon oil, preferably groundnut

Remove the corn kernels from the cob with a sharp knife or cleaver. You should end up with about 550 g (1¼ lb). If you are using tinned sweetcorn, empty the contents and drain thoroughly. Set aside half of the sweetcorn in a separate bowl. Combine the rest of the corn with the remaining ingredients, except the oil. Purée the mixture in a blender, then fold in the reserved corn.

Heat a frying-pan, preferably non-stick, add the oil and spoon in 2 tablespoons of the mixture. Cook the pancake over medium heat for 2–3 minutes or until golden brown on one side. Using a knife or spatula, turn the pancake over and cook the other side until crisp and golden. Remove, drain on kitchen paper and keep warm. Continue until you have used up all the mixture.

· CHINESE PANCAKES ·
Makes about 18 pancakes

These are simply flour-and-water pancakes with no seasonings or spices at all. As such, they blend perfectly with a variety of dishes such as Mu-Shu Vegetables (see p.114), and serve as the basis of other dishes such as Spring Onion Pancakes (see p.42). They are used like bread in the West. Once you have acquired the knack – practice, practice – they are easy to make. The unusual method of rolling 'double' pancakes is designed to ensure thinner, moister pancakes with less chance of being overcooked. Because they can be frozen, it is possible to make a batch many days, even weeks, in advance. Thaw thoroughly before steaming them. These pancakes can be used with practically any stir-fried dish which does not contain too much sauce.

275 g (10 oz) plain flour
225–250 ml (8–9 fl oz) very hot
water
2 tablespoons sesame oil

Put the flour into a large bowl. Stir the hot water gradually into the flour, mixing continuously with chopsticks or a fork until the water is fully incorporated. Add more water if the mixture seems dry. Remove the mixture from the bowl and knead it with your hands. Return it to the bowl, cover with a clean, damp tea towel and leave to rest for about 30 minutes.

After the resting period, take the dough out of the bowl and knead again for about 5 minutes, dusting with a little flour if sticky. Once the dough is smooth, form it into a roll about 46 cm (18 in) long and about 2.5 cm (1 in) in diameter. Take a knife and cut the roll into equal pieces. There should be about 18. Roll each piece into a ball.

Take 2 of the dough balls. Dip half of one ball into the sesame oil and place the oiled side on top of the other ball. Using a rolling pin, roll the 2 pancakes simultaneously into a circle about 15 cm (6 in) in diameter. It is important to roll double pancakes in this way because the resulting dough will remain moist inside and you will be able to roll them thinner, but avoid the risk of overcooking them later. Place a frying-pan or wok over a very low heat. Put the double pancake into the pan and cook until dried on one side. Flip the pancakes over and cook the other side. Remove from the pan, peel the 2 pancakes apart and set aside. Repeat this process until all the dough balls have been cooked.

Steam the pancakes to re-heat them, or alternatively you could wrap them tightly in a double sheet of foil and put into a pan containing 2.5 cm (1 in) of boiling water. Cover the pan, turn the heat down very low and simmer until they are re-heated. Don't be tempted to re-heat the pancakes in the oven as this will dry them out too much. If you want to freeze the cooked pancakes, wrap them tightly in freezer wrap first. When using pancakes which have been frozen, let them thaw in the fridge first before re-heating.

· SPRING ONION PANCAKES ·
Makes about 8 pancakes

Pancakes are familiar items in practically every cuisine. This particular type is popular in northern China, where winters are cold and harsh. They are slightly doughy and heavy but are nonetheless delicious and especially appropriate on cold winter days. In China, they are eaten with noodle soup or rice gruel in the mornings. Western habits and palates find them more suitable as starters or snacks with drinks. Pan-fried in oil with spring onion and sesame oil, these pancakes have an enticing, pungent aroma that gives the appetite an edge. They should be eaten while still warm. Although I like to use them as a starter, they are equally good as a snack with a bowl of hot soup or noodles. Use a non-stick pan and experiment with using as little oil as possible. The authentic original version is slightly too oily for my taste.

1 quantity pancake dough   ·   *1 tablespoon sesame oil*
(see p.41)   ·   *2–3 tablespoons oil, preferably*
8 spring onions, finely chopped · *groundnut*
1 tablespoon salt ·

Make up the pancake dough according to the recipe for Chinese Pancakes (see p.41). After the resting time, take the dough out of the bowl and knead it again for about 5 minutes, dusting with a little flour if sticky. Add the spring onions, salt and sesame oil, and knead the dough well.

Divide the dough into 8 equal pieces. Roll each piece into a circle about 15 cm (6 in) in diameter.

Place a non-stick frying-pan or wok over a low heat. Add enough oil to coat the bottom of the pan lightly. Put the pancakes into the pan, making sure the edges do not touch, and cook until the pancakes are crispy on one side. Flip them over and cook on the other side. You may have to do this in several batches. Cut each one into 6 wedges and serve at once.

· SUGAR WALNUTS ·
Serves 2–4

Walnuts, native to Asia, Europe and North America, hardly need an introduction. As might be expected, there are many ways of using them in the various cuisines of the world. Here, I have added the distinctive flavours of anise and cinnamon – walnuts are hearty enough to handle them, even though the blanching process has moderated the walnuts' slight bitterness. Cooking them in the syrup and allowing them to dry gives the walnuts a tasty coating and seals in the syrup flavours. Delicious served as a starter with drinks, these walnuts are also used in the recipe for Crispy Cabbage with Sugar Walnuts (see p.44), forming a classic combination of sweet and salty tastes, and crunchy and delicate crispness.

Once deep-fried, the walnuts can be stored in a tightly covered glass jar for at least a week. The recipe can easily be doubled.

100 g (4 oz) walnuts, shelled
300 ml (10 fl oz) oil, preferably groundnut, for deep-frying

Syrup
450 ml (15 fl oz) water

- *50 g (2 oz) sugar*
- *2 star anise*
- *1 cinnamon stick or Chinese cinnamon bark*
- *3 tablespoons clear honey*

Pre-heat the oven to its lowest temperature, then switch off.

Bring a saucepan of water to the boil. Add the walnuts and cook for 2 minutes to blanch. Drain the nuts in a colander or sieve.

Mix the syrup ingredients together in a pan. Combine the nuts with the syrup mixture and boil for 10 minutes or until the syrup mixture thickens. Remove the nuts with a slotted spoon, place on a baking tray and leave to dry in the oven for at least 2 hours.

Heat the oil in a deep-fat fryer or wok to moderate heat. Fry a batch of walnuts for about 2 minutes or until the walnuts turn dark brown (watch the heat to prevent burning). Remove the walnuts with a slotted spoon or strainer and lay them on a baking tray to cool. Deep-fry and drain the rest of the walnuts in the same way. Serve them warm with Crispy Cabbage or cold with drinks.

CRISPY CABBAGE WITH SUGAR WALNUTS

Serves 4

This is a popular vegetable starter in many Chinese restaurants in the UK, where it is known as 'Fried Seaweed'. In northern China, as I understand, there is a true seaweed dish to be had (which I have never eaten), but I should be very much surprised if it is available in Britain. In my experience, the 'seaweed' is shredded, dried and deep-fried fresh Chinese greens. The taste is fine but I prefer the version offered here, from the Sichuan Garden restaurant in Hong Kong. It uses a tinned preserved cabbage called 'red-in-snow' which is a pickled vegetable, traditional among the people of Chekiang and Kiangsu in northern China. It looks like turnip tops and both leaves and stalks are preserved. In the late winter or early spring, the red roots of the plant are often visible through the snow, hence its name. If you cannot find it, use Chinese green leaves, finely shredded and thoroughly dried in the oven. The key to the success of this dish is to be sure that the red-in-snow cabbage is thoroughly dried and the oil quite hot. Serve the dish at once.

185 g (6½ oz) tinned red-in-snow cabbage	•
300 ml (10 fl oz) oil, preferably	•

groundnut, for deep-frying
Sugar Walnuts (see p.43)

Rinse the cabbage in several changes of cold water. Place on a linen tea towel and squeeze out all the excess liquid.

Heat the oil in a deep-fat fryer or wok until it almost smokes. Deep-fry half of the cabbage for about 3 minutes or until crispy, then drain on kitchen paper. Repeat the process with the remaining cabbage. Mix the walnuts with the cabbage and serve at once.

▪ HOT AND SPICY WALNUTS ▪
Serves 4–6

This is a spicy, savoury way to prepare walnuts to be served either as a snack with drinks or as a crunchy addition to other stir-fry dishes. Prepared this way, the walnuts lend themselves to many uses; use your imagination and experiment with them. You may want to try them with Crispy Cabbage (see opposite) instead of using the sugar walnuts. If the walnuts get soft before they are used, you may re-crisp them by heating in a warm oven. They can be made ahead of time but should be eaten within a few days of their preparation. They do not keep for a long time because of the seasonings used in this recipe.

225 g (8 oz) walnuts, shelled
2 tablespoons chilli bean sauce
1 tablespoon finely chopped garlic
1 tablespoon finely chopped fresh ginger
3 tablespoons Chinese black rice vinegar or cider vinegar
2 tablespoons sugar
2 tablespoons dark soy sauce

2 tablespoons Chinese white rice vinegar or cider vinegar
750 ml (1¼ pints) water
450 ml (15 fl oz) oil, preferably groundnut, for deep-frying

Garnish
3 tablespoons finely chopped spring onions

Bring a saucepan of water to the boil. Add the walnuts and simmer for about 5 minutes to blanch. Drain the nuts in a colander or sieve, then pat dry with kitchen paper.

Combine all the remaining ingredients together in a saucepan. Add the walnuts and cook for about 20 minutes over high heat. Drain the nuts and spread them on a baking tray. Leave to dry for at least 2 hours.

Heat the oil in a deep-fat fryer or wok to a moderate heat. Fry some of the walnuts for about 3 minutes or until they turn deep brown and crispy. (Watch the heat to prevent burning.) You may have to deep-fry them in several batches. Remove the walnuts with a slotted spoon or strainer and drain on kitchen paper. Allow them to cool and become crisp before serving. Garnish with the spring onions.

VIETNAMESE-STYLE SPRING ROLLS

Makes about 25 small spring rolls

Spring rolls are very much a Chinese dish but, to my taste, the Vietnamese version is the best. They are made with rice paper wrappers instead of flour pancakes, and this renders them lighter and crisper. I like the traditional practice of wrapping the cooked spring rolls in a fresh lettuce leaf with mint, basil or fresh coriander leaves and dipping them in a spicy peanut sauce. Such spring rolls are a splendid opener to any meal. The rice paper wrappers can be found in Chinese or oriental grocers. They are dry and must be gently soaked before using them. Handle them with care as they are quite fragile. When deep-frying the spring rolls, do not crowd them in the pan as they tend to stick.

1 packet rice paper wrappers
450 ml (15 fl oz) oil, preferably groundnut, for deep-frying

Stuffing
50 g (2 oz) bean thread (transparent) noodles
50 g (2 oz) carrots, finely shredded
100 g (4 oz) mangetout, finely shredded
3 tablespoons finely chopped spring onions

1 teaspoon sesame oil
2 tablespoons light soy sauce
1 teaspoon Chinese rice wine or dry sherry

To serve
225 g (8 oz) iceberg lettuce
assorted sprigs of basil, mint or coriander, or a combination of all three
Spicy Peanut Sauce (see p.48)

For the stuffing, soak the noodles in a large bowl of warm water for 15 minutes. When they are soft, drain and discard the water. Cut the noodles into 7.5 cm (3 in) lengths, using scissors or a knife.

In a large bowl, mix the noodles with the carrots, mangetout, spring onions, sesame oil, light soy sauce and rice wine.

To make the spring rolls, fill a large bowl with warm water and dip one of the rice paper wrappers in the water to soften. Remove and drain on a linen tea towel. Put about 2 tablespoons of the filling on each softened rice paper wrapper. (See drawings below.) Fold in each side and then roll up tightly. They will seal by themselves. You should have a roll about 7.5 cm (3 in) long, a little like a small sausage. Repeat the procedure until you have used up all the filling.

Heat the oil in a deep-fat fryer or large wok until it is hot. Deep-fry the spring rolls, a few at a time, until golden brown, about 2 minutes. Drain on kitchen paper. Serve at once with lettuce leaves, herb sprigs and Spicy Peanut Sauce (see over).

· SPICY PEANUT SAUCE ·

Makes enough for about 25 small spring rolls

Dipping sauces are common in all Far Eastern cuisines. Here is a tasty Southeast Asian version with a peanut flavour, commonly used with spring rolls. You may adjust the chilli oil to suit your own palate. This sauce may be made well ahead of time.

1 tablespoon light soy sauce	1 teaspoon chilli oil
2 tablespoons Chinese white rice vinegar or cider vinegar	2 tablespoons water
½ teaspoon finely chopped garlic	1 teaspoon sugar
3 tablespoons roasted peanuts, coarsely chopped	

Combine all the ingredients together in a small bowl, mixing them thoroughly. Leave the dipping sauce to stand for at least 10 minutes before using.

· NORTHERN CHINESE VEGETABLE POTSTICKERS ·

Makes about 20 dumplings

Potstickers are a form of dumpling and, in northern China, they are a speciality in restaurants and a staple in home kitchens. To this day, making them is a family affair and social occasion, with Sunday mornings before the big lunch meal devoted to their preparation. In general, dumplings may be shallow-fried, boiled, poached or steamed. One very popular way to make them is to shallow-fry in oil and water until they literally stick to the pan, a method I like best of all. Properly done, it produces true potsticker dumplings that are crisp on the bottom, soft on the top and juicy inside. The goal is to have a contrast of textures and flavours.

In China, potsticker dumplings usually include minced pork. But they are equally satisfying as a vegetarian dish. Try to obtain the Chinese preserved vegetables and Chinese chives; they add an excellent flavour to the dumplings. You may substitute ordinary chives, but there is really no substitute for the preserved vegetables. Make your own dipping sauce with chilli oil, dark soy sauce and Chinese white rice vinegar or cider vinegar.

Potsticker dumplings may be frozen uncooked and can be transferred directly from the freezer to the pan; just cook them a little longer than usual. Ready-made potsticker wrappers can be found in Chinese grocers if you choose not to make your own.

1 packet potsticker wrappers, bought or made according to the recipe below

Dough
150 g (5 oz) plain flour
120 ml (4 fl oz) very hot water

Stuffing
100 g (4 oz) fresh or frozen peas
50 g (2 oz) Sichuan preserved vegetables, finely chopped
2 tablespoons finely chopped garlic

225 g (8 oz) bok choy, finely chopped
225 g (8 oz) Chinese chives, coarsely chopped
¼ teaspoon salt
a pinch of freshly ground pepper
2 tablespoons rice wine or dry sherry
1 tablespoon dark soy sauce
2 teaspoons sugar
3 tablespoons oil, preferably groundnut
150 ml (5 fl oz) water

If you are making the dough, put the flour into a large bowl and gradually stir in the hot water, mixing continuously with a fork or chopsticks until most of the water is incorporated. Add more water if the mixture seems dry. Remove the dough from the bowl and knead with your hands until smooth. This should take about 5 minutes. Put the dough back into the bowl, cover with a clean, damp tea towel and leave to rest for about 20 minutes.

While the dough is resting, make the stuffing. If you are using fresh peas, blanch them in a pan of boiling water for 4 minutes or 2 minutes if they are frozen. Rinse the Sichuan preserved vegetables several times in cold water and blot them dry.

Heat a wok or large frying-pan over high heat and add 1 tablespoon of the oil. Add the stuffing ingredients and stir-fry for 5 minutes or until the mixture is dry. Remove the mixture to a bowl and allow the stuffing ingredients to cool thoroughly.

After the resting time, take the dough out of the bowl and knead it again for about 5 minutes, dusting with a little flour if sticky. Once the dough is smooth, form into a roll about 23 cm (9 in) long and about 2.5 cm (1 in) in diameter. Take a knife and cut the roll into 18 equal pieces.

Roll each piece of dough into a small ball, then roll each ball into a small, round, flat 'pancake' about 6 cm (2½ in) in diameter. Arrange the rounds on a lightly floured tray and cover with damp kitchen paper to keep them from drying out until required.

Put about 1 tablespoon of the filling in the centre of each pancake, then fold in half. Moisten the edges with water and pinch together with your fingers. Pleat around the edge, pinching to seal well. Transfer the finished dumplings to the floured tray and keep it covered with a damp cloth until you have filled all the dumplings in this way.

Heat a frying-pan (preferably non-stick) over a high heat until hot and add 1 tablespoon of the oil. Place the dumplings, flat side down, into the pan. Turn down the heat and cook for about 2 minutes until lightly browned. (You may need to cook the dumplings in two batches.) Add the 150 ml (5 fl oz) of water, cover the pan tightly and cook for about 12 minutes or until most of the liquid is absorbed. Uncover the pan and continue to cook for a further 2 minutes. Remove the dumplings and serve.

Place three bowls on the table, containing Chinese white rice vinegar, chilli oil and dark soy sauce. Let each person concoct their own dipping sauce by mixing these three items exactly to their taste.

· WINTER VEGETABLE FRITTERS ·
Serves 2–4

These vegetable fritters (similar to pancakes), served warm or at room temperature, are an appetizing starter for any meal. You may substitute other vegetables as long as they are firm, such as cucumbers or courgettes. The key ingredient in this version is fresh waterchestnuts – try to obtain them, for they add a special sweetness and texture to the fritters. Served with a simple green salad, these vegetable fritters also make a delicious light lunch.

100 g (4 oz) carrots	*3 eggs, beaten*
100 g (4 oz) fresh or tinned waterchestnuts	*2 teaspoons salt*
	2 teaspoons baking powder
100 g (4 oz) cabbage	*2 teaspoons sugar*
1 small onion	*1 teaspoon freshly ground black pepper*
6 tablespoons plain flour	
1 tablespoon cornflour	*3–4 tablespoons oil, preferably groundnut*

Finely chop the carrots, waterchestnuts, cabbage and onion. Lightly blend all the ingredients, except the oil, in a food processor or food mill for a few seconds. Do not use a blender.

Heat a frying-pan or wok and add the oil. Spoon in 3 tablespoons of the mixture to make a 10 cm (4 in) wide pancake and fry for 2–3 minutes or until golden brown on one side. Using a knife or spatula, turn the pancake over and cook the other side until crispy and golden. Continue this process until you have used up all the mixture. Cut the fritters into wedges and serve.

· C R I S P Y W O N T O N S ·

Makes 30–35 wontons

Wontons stuffed with tasty fillings of flavourful vegetables are universally appreciated. This is a vegetarian version of the traditional Chinese treat with a filling of carrots, cabbage and bean sprouts, with some beancurd for body. These wontons are delicious with hoisin sauce or, if you prefer, a dipping sauce made with your own combination of chilli oil, white rice wine vinegar and light soy sauce. These wontons are ideal with drinks or as a starter.

Do *not* make them too far ahead of time. Because they are made with a moisture-laden vegetable stuffing, the wonton skins will soften in an unpalatable way if they are allowed to stand for a long time. If possible, make and serve them straight away.

1 packet wonton skins
(about 30–35)
450 ml (15 fl oz) oil, preferably
groundnut, for deep-frying
hoisin sauce, for dipping

Filling
1 tablespoon oil, preferably
groundnut
50 g (2 oz) carrots, finely shredded
100 g (4 oz) cabbage, finely
shredded

50 g (2 oz) bean sprouts
2 tablespoons finely chopped
garlic
1 tablespoon dark soy sauce
3 tablespoons mashed beancurd
1 teaspoon sugar
½ teaspoon salt
1 teaspoon sesame oil
½ teaspoon freshly ground black
pepper

For the filling, heat a wok or large frying-pan and add the oil. When moderately hot, add the carrots, cabbage, bean sprouts and garlic and stir-fry for 1 minute. Set aside to cool thoroughly.

Combine the cooled vegetables with the rest of the filling ingredients and mix well. Using a teaspoon, put a small amount of filling in the centre of each wonton skin. (See drawings opposite.) Bring up two opposite corners, dampen the edges with a little water and pinch them together to make a triangle. Fold over the bottom two corners so they overlap, and press together. The filling should be well sealed in.

Heat the oil in a deep-fat fryer or large wok until hot. Deep-fry the filled wontons in several batches. Drain on kitchen paper. Serve at once with hoisin sauce.

· AUBERGINES WITH SESAME SAUCE ·
Serves 4

This is a very easy and delicious way to prepare aubergines. Try to obtain the smaller, more delicately flavoured Chinese aubergines if you can. The cooking process produces sweet, tender and moist aubergine flesh, and increases its receptivity to the classic Sichuan sauce: garlic, ginger and spring onions. This dish makes a delicious starter and, as it is served cold, may be made hours in advance. The sauce, however, should not be poured over the cooked aubergines until just before serving.

750 g (1½ lb) Chinese or ordinary aubergines

Sauce
1 tablespoon sesame paste
½ teaspoon roasted Sichuan peppercorns (see p.24)
2 tablespoons sesame oil
2 teaspoons chilli oil

- *2 teaspoons sugar*
- *1 teaspoon Chinese white rice vinegar or cider vinegar*
- *½ teaspoon finely chopped garlic*
- *½ teaspoon finely chopped fresh ginger*
- *2 tablespoons finely chopped spring onions*
- *1 tablespoon dark soy sauce*

Pre-heat the oven to 200°C/400°F/Gas 6. Put the aubergines in a roasting tin and bake in the oven for about 30 minutes if they are the Chinese variety or 45 minutes if they are the larger variety. They should be charred outside and tender inside. Allow them to cool thoroughly.

Peel the aubergines and shred the flesh or cut into strips. Arrange the aubergines on a serving plate.

Mix all the sauce ingredients together in a small bowl. Just before serving, pour the sauce over the aubergine.

· S P I C Y   K O R E A N   K I M C H I ·
Makes about 450 g (1 lb)

Pickled vegetables are a speciality in Chinese and Southeast Asian cuisines. This is understandable, given the abundance of vegetables on the one hand and the absence of refrigeration (until quite recently) on the other. Necessity generated inventiveness and imagination to preserve the foods in a palatable way. Korean meals almost always include a pickled vegetable, 'kimchi' as it is called generically, to stimulate the palate and as a contrast to less fiery foods. In the West, we use our pickled dishes more sparingly, serving them on picnics or with cold platters. In this adaptation of Korean kimchi, I follow the traditional method of fermentation without the use of vinegar. The leaves develop a slightly sour taste enlivened by chilli – if you find it too hot, reduce the amount of chilli. Pickled cabbage is sold in glass jars in specialist food shops but it is usually full of preservatives and monosodium glutamate. I urge you to make your own; it is quite simple, can be prepared in advance, and keeps for weeks in the fridge.

450 g (1 lb) Chinese leaves
2 tablespoons salt
1.2 litres (2 pints) cold water
600 ml (1 pint) very hot water

Pickling mixture
1 tablespoon finely chopped garlic
1 tablespoon finely chopped fresh ginger

- *1 tablespoon finely chopped spring onions*
- *2 teaspoons finely chopped dried chilli*
- *2 teaspoons sugar*
- *1 tablespoon salt*

Separate the Chinese leaves and sprinkle them with the salt. Pour in the cold water and leave to stand in a cool place for 8 hours or overnight. Rinse the cabbage well and squeeze out the excess liquid.

Boil the water and pour over the pickling mixture. Mix well and combine with the Chinese leaves. Put the leaves with the pickling mixture into a large glass bowl. You may have to cut the leaves in half to make them fit. Cover the kimchi with cling film and leave in a cool place for about 2 days. Drain and cut the leaves into bite-sized pieces. Pack into a glass jar until ready to serve.

JAPANESE-STYLE MARINATED MUSHROOMS

Serves 4

What could be easier than a dish that requires no cooking? Well, almost no cooking: the marinade must be heated and it in turn 'cooks' the mushrooms overnight.

450 g (1 lb) small button mushrooms

Marinade
150 ml (5 fl oz) sake, rice wine or dry sherry
2 tablespoons light soy sauce
2 teaspoons sugar

1 tablespoon Chinese white rice vinegar or cider vinegar
½ teaspoon salt

Garnish
2 tablespoons finely chopped spring onions

Place the marinade ingredients in a small pan and simmer for about 5 minutes. Allow to cool thoroughly. Combine the cooled marinade with the whole mushrooms and leave to marinate overnight.

When ready to serve the mushrooms, drain them and discard the marinade. Garnish with the spring onions.

· CRUNCHY RADISH SALAD ·

Serves 2–4

Looking like long, overgrown white carrots, these radishes are a staple in Chinese cookery. I have seen them referred to as icicle radish, Chinese turnip and rettish. In Britain, they are known as mooli or Chinese white radish. They are never eaten raw in China, but I enjoy their crunchy texture, especially in salads such as this. They have a mild peppery taste which is muted by cooking them; in this recipe, they are salted to remove the bite. Once this is done, the radishes lend themselves very well to other spices and seasonings, as in this Chinese dressing of soy sauce, sugar, pepper and sesame oil. Remember that the cool crunchy bite of Chinese radishes works well with Western-type dressings, so do experiment. If you cannot obtain the Chinese version, substitute ordinary radishes but cut them in half to show off their whiteness and expose them to the dressing. (Salting ordinary radishes is optional.)

350 g (12 oz) Chinese white radish (mooli)
2 teaspoons salt

Dressing
¼ teaspoon roasted Sichuan peppercorns (see p.24)

1 tablespoon light soy sauce
1 teaspoon sugar
1 tablespoon sesame oil

Cut the radish into 7.5 cm (3 in) long, 5 mm (¼ in) thick pieces. Salt the pieces, toss to mix thoroughly and set aside for 20 minutes. Rinse the radish and pat dry with kitchen paper.

For the dressing, combine all the ingredients and pour over the radish. Mix thoroughly and serve.

CHAPTER TWO

SOUPS

Soup is excellent either to start a meal or as a meal in itself. In China and Southeast Asia, soups are often served as part of a meal, as one of the courses on the table; it also serves as a beverage. In this book, there are two types of soups: hearty and rich, such as Fiery Sichuan Soup or Sizzling Rice Soup; and light, brothy ones such as Tangy Tomato Soup with Lemon Grass or Steamed Vegetable Soup. They may be used either as part of an oriental menu or in your everyday meals. Many are simple and easy to put together, especially if you have the stock already prepared.

The key to any good soup is the stock. It is virtually impossible to have a good soup without it. Although it takes a little effort and work to make a good stock, the rewards make it well worthwhile. Many of the soups in this book are based on a vegetable stock. Japanese recipes traditionally use 'dashi', a fish-based stock, but vegetable stock can also be used.

VEGETABLE STOCK

Good stock is essential to all cuisines. This is especially true for one that relies upon vegetables. Because of its lightness, flavour and versatility, stock should be considered a staple like salt, cooking oil or soy sauce. There are commercially prepared tinned or cubed stocks but many of them are inferior in quality, being too salty or containing additives and colourants.

Vegetarian cooking, however, can present a problem when it comes to stock. In the absence of poultry, fish or meat, it is difficult to prepare a rich stock, the foundation of any cuisine. Vegetable stocks tend to be comparatively weak and lack robustness. Even in China, the custom has been to add the additive monosodium glutamate to vegetable stock. Another popular vegetable stock employs the peppery bite of white radish to impart body to it. With my colleague Gordon Wing, I have experimented and found that cooking the vegetables in oil *before* simmering helps to impart flavour to the stock. Gordon suggests using dried Chinese mushrooms to add richness and depth.

Try to make your own, as the best stock is home-made. I usually make up a large batch of it and freeze in smaller portions for future use, but if you find the portions too large for your needs, cut the recipe in half.

Remember – *stock is the foundation of all good cooking*. Here are a few rules to remember when making stock.

Stock should simmer. Never leave it to boil because that will result in a cloudy and heavy stock. Good flavour and digestibility come with a clear stock.

Use a deep heavy pan so the liquid covers all the solids and evaporation is slow.

Simmer on low heat and gently skim the stock every now and then to remove any impurities.

Strain the stock slowly through several layers of muslin or a fine mesh strainer.

Allow the stock to cool thoroughly before freezing.

· BASIC VEGETABLE STOCK ·

Makes about 4.5 litres (8 pints)

*25 g (1 oz) Chinese dried
mushrooms (optional)
900 g (2 lb) carrots
4 celery sticks
900 g (2 lb) onions
4 leeks
225 g (8 oz) shallots
2 tablespoons oil, preferably
groundnut*

- *6 spring onions*
- *6 slices fresh ginger*
- *8 garlic cloves, crushed*
- *1 tablespoon black peppercorns*
- *1 tablespoon Sichuan peppercorns*
- *4 bay leaves*
- *2 tablespoons salt*
- *4.5 litres (8 pints) water*
- *3 tablespoons light soy sauce*

If you are using dried mushrooms, soak them in warm water for 20 minutes. Drain, squeeze out any excess liquid and coarsely chop the mushroom caps and stalks.

Coarsely chop the carrots, celery and onions. Wash, cut and discard the green part of the leeks and coarsely chop the white portion. Peel the shallots but leave them whole.

Heat a large pan or wok over moderate heat and add the oil. Put in the spring onions, ginger, garlic and shallots, and stir-fry for 1 minute. Then add the carrots, celery, leeks and onions and continue to cook for 5 minutes. Put all the vegetables and the rest of the ingredients into a very large pan. Cover them with the cold water and bring to simmering point.

Using a large, flat spoon, skim off the foam as it rises to the top; this will take about 5 minutes. Heat the stock until it is almost boiling. Reduce the heat to moderate and simmer for about 2 hours.

Strain the stock through a large colander, then through a very fine mesh strainer. Leave to cool thoroughly. It is now ready to be used or transferred to containers and frozen for future use.

SOFT BEANCURD AND SPINACH SOUP

Serves 4

This simple but delicious and nutritious soup is easy to prepare and one you would often find on the table in China. Use *soft* beancurd: its custard-like texture and mild flavour work with the sugar to neutralize the metallic edge of the spinach. The bean thread noodles give substance to this warming soup.

50 g (2 oz) bean thread (transparent) noodles	2 tablespoons light soy sauce
750 g (1½ lb) fresh spinach	3 tablespoons rice wine or dry sherry
225 g (8 oz) soft beancurd	2 teaspoons sugar
1.2 litres (2 pints) vegetable stock	½ teaspoon salt

Soak the noodles in a large bowl of warm water for 15 minutes. When soft, drain them and discard the water. Cut the noodles into 7.5 cm (3 in) lengths using scissors or a knife. Remove the stalks from the spinach and wash the leaves well. Gently cut the beancurd into 2.5 cm (1 in) cubes.

Put the stock into a pan and bring to simmering point. Add the bean thread noodles and simmer for 2 minutes. Add the spinach and the rest of the ingredients except the beancurd. Simmer for 2 minutes, then gently put in the beancurd. Continue to simmer the soup for a further 2 minutes to heat the beancurd through. Serve at once.

TANGY TOMATO SOUP WITH LEMON GRASS
Serves 2–4

This Thai–Chinese recipe is so intertwined that it is difficult to differentiate the various contributors. The Thai cuisine specializes in hot, tangy, spicy soups that are refreshing and stimulating. The Chinese cuisine includes many soups that are as beautiful as they are flavoursome, providing the eggflower motif – attractive strands of lace-like white of egg. The lemon grass, refreshing and aromatic, is used in both cuisines. This impressive yet easy to make soup could be served at the grandest dinner. Alternatively, simply add blanched rice noodles to the soup and it becomes a meal in itself.

1.2 litres (2 pints) vegetable stock
450 g (1 lb) fresh or tinned tomatoes
1 fresh lemon grass stalk or 1 tablespoon finely chopped lemon rind
1½ teaspoons salt
2 teaspoons sugar
1 tablespoon lemon juice

2 tablespoons finely chopped spring onions
1 small chilli, sliced
1 tablespoon finely chopped fresh coriander
1 egg white
2 teaspoons sesame oil

Garnish
fresh coriander leaves

Put the stock in a pan and bring to simmering point. If using fresh tomatoes, skin, seed and cut the flesh into 2.5 cm (1 in) cubes. If using tinned tomatoes, chop into small chunks. Peel the lemon grass stalk to the tender whitish centre and finely chop it.

Add the salt, sugar, lemon juice, spring onions, chilli and coriander to the simmering stock and stir to mix well. Add the tomatoes and simmer for 3 minutes. Lightly beat the egg white and combine with the sesame oil in a small bowl. Pour the egg white mixture into the soup in a very slow, thin stream. Using a chopstick or fork, pull the egg slowly into strands. (I have found that stirring the egg white in a figure-of-eight works quite well.) Garnish with the coriander leaves and serve.

· SIZZLING RICE SOUP ·

Serves 4

This soup delights not only the eye, the nose and the palate, but the ear as well. I always enjoy making it because, as well as the dramatic sizzling, it is so full of flavour and easy to do. The ingredients are simple, requiring little preparation, much of which can be done ahead of time. Rice cakes are easy to make, once you have prepared them a few times. The key point to remember is that the oil used for deep-frying the pieces must be *very* hot to ensure that they become very crispy and not greasy – almost like dried popcorn. While the soup itself re-heats well, the rice cake pieces must be deep-fried just before serving.

25 g (1 oz) Chinese dried mushrooms
15 g (½ oz) Chinese dried wood ears
1.2 litres (2 pints) vegetable stock
450 g (1 lb) soft beancurd, cut into 1 cm (½ in) cubes
4 tablespoons finely chopped spring onions
3 tablespoons rice wine or dry sherry

2 tablespoons light soy sauce
2 teaspoons chilli oil
½ teaspoon salt
Rice Cake (see opposite)
600 ml (1 pint) oil, preferably groundnut, for deep-frying

Garnish
fresh coriander leaves

In separate bowls, soak the dried mushrooms and wood ears in warm water for 20 minutes. Drain them and squeeze out any excess liquid. Trim off the tough stalks and shred the mushroom caps and wood ears into 5 cm (2 in) strips.

Bring the stock to simmering point in a large pan. Add the remaining soup ingredients, setting aside the rice cake and oil for deep-frying. Simmer for 20 minutes before transferring the soup to a large serving bowl.

Meanwhile, heat the oil in a large frying-pan or wok until it is nearly smoking. Drop in a grain of rice to test the heat – the rice should bubble all over and immediately come up to the surface.

Cut the rice cake into pieces and deep-fry for about 1–2 minutes until they puff up and brown slightly. Remove immediately with a slotted spoon and drain on kitchen paper. Quickly transfer the pieces to a platter and slide them into the soup. It should sizzle dramatically. Garnish with the fresh coriander leaves and serve at once.

▪ R I C E   C A K E ▪
Makes a 23 cm (9 in) rice cake

225 g (8 oz) long-grain white rice	▪	*2 teaspoons oil, preferably*
600 ml (1 pint) water	▪	*groundnut*

Wash the rice and put into a 23 cm (9 in) wide, heavy pan with the water. Bring the water to the boil over high heat. Turn the heat down as low as possible, cover and cook the rice for about 45 minutes. The rice should form a heavy crust on the base of the pan. Remove all the loose surface rice, leaving the thick crust. (This loose rice can be used for making any of the fried rice recipes in Chapter Eight.)

Dribble the oil evenly over the top of the rice cake and cook over a very low heat for 5 minutes. The cake should lift off easily at this point. If it is still sticky, add another teaspoon of oil and continue to cook until the whole cake comes loose. Put the cake onto a plate until required.

Once cooked, it can be left at room temperature for several days. Do *not* cover the rice cake, as moisture will form and make it soggy. Let the rice cake dry out. It is then ready to be cut into several pieces, deep-fried and put into the Sizzling Rice Soup (see previous recipe). As a simple snack, break it into chunks and eat hot with a sprinkling of salt.

· JAPANESE SEAWEED SOUP ·

Serves 4

This light, rather austere soup is typical of Japanese cookery. Seaweed is high in protein and evokes the essence of the sea, and as nothing should mask this delicate, rich flavour, the soup is kept very simple. The dried seaweed is well worth searching for. Once the stock is made and the seaweed soaked, the recipe can be quickly put together in a matter of minutes. The traditional version uses *dashi*, a fish-based stock, but vegetable stock is equally good.

3 sheets 15 × 20 cm (6 × 8 in) dried wakame seaweed
1.2 litres (2 pints) vegetable stock
rind of 1 lemon or lime, cut into thin matchsticks
½ teaspoon salt
2 tablespoons light soy sauce

Soak the seaweed for 20 minutes in warm water or until soft. Drain and cut it into thin shreds.

Bring the stock to simmering point in a large pan. Add the lemon rind, salt and light soy sauce and continue to simmer for another 2 minutes. Remove the soup from the heat and add the seaweed. Serve at once.

OPPOSITE: **Vietnamese-style Spring Rolls with Spicy Peanut Sauce**
(pages 46–48)

LIGHT LUNCH
Button Mushrooms in Soy Sauce *(page 114)*
Thai Aromatic Fried Rice *(page 189)*
Green and White Jade Salad *(page 85)*

FAMILY MEAL
Tangy Tomato Soup with Lemon Grass *(page 61)*
Chow Mein *(page 168)*
Crispy Vegetable Stir-Fry *(page 131)*
Malaysian Coconut Custard *(page 206)*

INDONESIAN
CAULIFLOWER SOUP

Serves 2–4

Cauliflower is a delicately flavoured vegetable with a firm texture. In a soup such as this, it retains its pleasing characteristics while combining well with the distinctive flavours of coriander and cumin. The egg noodles add substance to the dish.

In its original Indonesian version, the soup is usually made with beef stock, but I prefer to use the lighter vegetable stock. Served with fresh bread (toasted perhaps) and a green salad, this hearty soup is a meal in itself.

450 g (1 lb) cauliflower
1 tablespoon oil, preferably groundnut
1 tablespoon finely chopped garlic
1 small onion, finely chopped
1½ teaspoons salt
¼ teaspoon freshly ground black pepper
1 teaspoon ground coriander

2 teaspoons ground cumin
1.2 litres (2 pints) vegetable stock
100 g (4 oz) dried or fresh egg noodles

Garnish
1 tablespoon finely chopped fresh coriander

Cut the cauliflower into florets about 2.5–4 cm (1–1½ in) wide.

Heat a wok or large frying-pan and add the oil. Put in the garlic, onion, ½ teaspoon of the salt, pepper, coriander and cumin and stir-fry for about 2 minutes. Add the stock and cauliflower and simmer the mixture for 20 minutes or until the cauliflower is cooked.

Add the noodles to the simmering soup and cook for 8–10 minutes for dried noodles or 4–5 minutes for fresh noodles.

Add the remaining salt and give the soup a good stir. Transfer to a soup tureen and serve at once garnished with the coriander.

OPPOSITE: **Sizzling Rice Soup** *(page 62)*

· SWEETCORN AND GINGER SOUP ·

Serves 4–6

Sweetcorn soup with crab or chicken has become a very popular dish in many Chinese restaurants in the West. It is not truly Chinese but rather reflects a blend of Eastern and Western traditions. Here is my version of the soup, a lighter vegetarian one that contains the zest of fresh ginger to enliven it. I prefer to use fresh sweetcorn, as I find the starch used in the tinned variety tends to make the soup heavy. The milk in the recipe is definitely borrowed from the Western tradition; for a richer taste, use cream. This is an elegant starter for any dinner party.

750 g (1½ lb) fresh sweetcorn on the cob, or 425 g (15 oz) tinned sweetcorn kernels
1 egg, beaten
½ teaspoon sesame oil
1 tablespoon oil, preferably groundnut
1 tablespoon finely chopped fresh ginger
1.2 litres (2 pints) vegetable stock
2 tablespoons rice wine or dry sherry

150 ml (5 fl oz) milk
2 teaspoons salt
½ teaspoon freshly ground white pepper
1 tablespoon sugar

Garnish
1 tablespoon finely chopped spring onions

If you are using fresh sweetcorn, remove the kernels with a sharp knife or cleaver – you should end up with about 425 g (15 oz). Mix the egg and sesame oil together in a small bowl and set aside.

Heat a large pan until moderately hot. Add the oil and ginger and stir-fry for 30 seconds. Add the rest of the ingredients, except the corn, egg mixture and spring onions. Bring the mixture to the boil and add the corn. Simmer for 15 minutes, uncovered, and then allow it to cool slightly.

Purée the soup in a blender or food mill until light and creamy. Return the soup to the pan and bring to a slow simmer. Add the egg mixture, stirring all the time. For serving, transfer the soup to a tureen or individual bowls and garnish with the spring onions.

SPINACH AND EGG-RIBBON SOUP

Serves 4

When a soup appears as beautiful as it tastes, it is safe to assume a Japanese influence, as with this light soup. For a truly authentic flavour it should be made with *dashi*, but a good vegetable stock produces a fine soup. The attractive 'egg ribbons' are made by pulling or stretching the egg strands with a fork or chopsticks as you pour them slowly into the soup.

100 g (4 oz) fresh spinach
1.2 litres (2 pints) vegetable stock
2 eggs, beaten
1 teaspoon fresh ginger juice (see p.17)

1 teaspoon salt
1 tablespoon sake, rice wine or dry sherry
1 teaspoon cornflour mixed with 1 teaspoon water

Remove the stalks from the spinach and wash the leaves well. Blanch them for a few seconds in a pan of boiling water until they are just wilted. Freshen the leaves in cold water to prevent further cooking.

Put the stock into a pan and bring to simmering point. Lightly beat the eggs and combine them with the ginger juice. Add the salt, sake and blended cornflour to the simmering stock, and stir to mix well. Pour in the egg mixture in a very slow, thin stream. Using a chopstick or fork, pull the egg slowly into strands. Drain the spinach and add to the hot soup before serving.

· STEAMED VEGETABLE SOUP ·

Serves 4–6

This is one of my favourite soups. In China, it is called 'double-boiled' or 'double-steamed', the name deriving from the cooking technique used. The prepared ingredients are put in a casserole containing a boiling rich stock; then the casserole is sealed and placed in a steamer – a double cooking process that creates a flavourful soup. It is popular among all Chinese, and in Hong Kong it is made from various ingredients, such as shark fins, pigeons, bird's nests, chicken and, as in the recipe, vegetables. Because vegetables cook quickly, this takes little more than half an hour to cook to full flavour and the result is a clear soup, rather like a rich consommé. It makes a splendid first course for dinner parties or can be served as part of a family meal.

25 g (1 oz) *Chinese dried mushrooms*
100 g (4 oz) *Chinese white radish (mooli)*
100 g (4 oz) *fresh or tinned waterchestnuts*
2 *eggs, beaten*
1 *teaspoon salt*

1 *teaspoon sesame oil*
1 *tablespoon oil, preferably groundnut*
1.2 *litres (2 pints) vegetable stock*

Garnish
watercress leaves

Soak the dried mushrooms in warm water for 20 minutes until they are soft. Squeeze the excess liquid from the mushrooms and remove and discard the stalks. Leave the caps whole.

Peel and cut the Chinese radish into 7.5 cm (3 in) long pieces. If you are using fresh waterchestnuts, peel them; if you are using tinned waterchestnuts, drain well and rinse in cold water. Thinly slice the waterchestnuts. Beat the eggs, ½ teaspoon of the salt and the sesame oil together in a small bowl.

Heat a wok or frying-pan until hot and add the oil. Pour in the egg mixture and cook until it sets. Remove the omelette and leave to cool. Cut it into 1 cm (½ in) shreds.

Set a rack into a wok or deep pan. Fill with 6 cm (2½ in) of water and bring it to the boil. Heat the stock in another large pan until it is almost boiling and then pour the stock into a heatproof glass or china casserole. Add the radish, waterchestnuts, egg shreds, mushrooms and remaining salt to the stock. Cover and put the casserole on the rack, then cover the wok or deep pan tightly with a lid or foil. You now have a casserole within a steamer, hence the name 'double-boil'. Reduce the heat and steam gently for 35 minutes or until the radish is cooked. Replenish the hot water from time to time. An alternative method is to simply simmer the soup very slowly in a conventional pan, but the resulting taste will be quite different.

When the soup is cooked, it can be served immediately or cooled and stored in the fridge or freezer to be re-heated when required. Garnish the soup with the watercress just before serving.

▪ FIERY SICHUAN SOUP ▪
Serves 4

One of the great virtues of Chinese and most oriental cookery is their adaptability when confronted with new influences. This hot and spicy soup, now so popular in the West, is traditionally made with pork but, when dried mushrooms and cloud ears (black fungus) are substituted, the soup retains its excellent qualities and remains a substantial and nutritious meal. Do try to obtain the dried mushrooms and cloud ears – their textures are quite special.

50 g (2 oz) bean thread (transparent) noodles
15 g (½ oz) Chinese dried mushrooms
15 g (½ oz) Chinese dried cloud ears (black fungus)
100 g (4 oz) bamboo shoots, shredded
1 egg, beaten
2 teaspoons sesame oil
1.2 litres (2 pints) vegetable stock
1 tablespoon finely chopped fresh ginger

- *2 tablespoons tomato purée*
- *1 tablespoon light soy sauce*
- *2 tablespoons dark soy sauce*
- *2 tablespoons chilli oil*
- *1 tablespoon black rice vinegar or cider vinegar*
- *2 teaspoons freshly ground black pepper*

Garnish
3 tablespoons finely chopped spring onions

Soak the noodles in a large bowl of warm water for 15 minutes. When they are soft, drain and discard the water. Cut the noodles into 7.5 cm (3 in) lengths, using scissors or a knife.

Soak the dried mushrooms and cloud ears in separate bowls of warm water for 20 minutes until soft. Squeeze the excess liquid from the mushrooms and remove and discard the stalks. Rinse the cloud ears in cold water, drain well and leave whole. Shred the mushroom caps finely. Finely shred the bamboo shoots. Beat the egg and sesame oil together in a small bowl.

Bring the stock to simmering point in a large pan. Add the mushrooms, cloud ears, bamboo shoots, noodles and the rest of the ingredients, except the egg mixture and spring onions. Simmer for 5 minutes.

Finally, pour the beaten egg mixture into the soup in a steady stream. Pull the egg into strands with a fork or chopsticks. Garnish with the spring onions and pour the soup into a large tureen or individual bowls. Serve at once.

· FRAGRANT NOODLE SOUP ·
Serves 2–4

Egg noodles are a simple and comforting food – plain, homely, nutritious and satisfying. Combined with soup, their virtues are magnified, and when we add a touch of Southeast Asian zest – lime juice – the result is a wholesome soup that can serve as a light lunch for two or as a starter for any meal.

225 g (8 oz) fresh or dried egg noodles
1.2 litres (2 pints) vegetable stock
2 tablespoons finely chopped spring onions
1 tablespoon finely chopped fresh coriander

- *100 g (4 oz) celery, finely chopped*
- *2 teaspoons sesame oil*
- *1 tablespoon chilli oil*
- *2 tablespoons light soy sauce*
- *1 tablespoon lime juice*
- *2 teaspoons sugar*

If you are using fresh noodles, blanch them for 3–5 minutes in a large pan of boiling water, then immerse in cold water. If you are using dried noodles, cook in boiling water for 4–5 minutes. Drain the noodles, then cool in cold water until required.

Put the stock into a pan and bring to simmering point. Add the rest of the ingredients and simmer for 5 minutes. Drain the noodles and add them to the soup. Bring the soup back to simmering point and serve at once.

SOUTHEAST ASIAN VEGETABLE SOUP

Serves 4–6

I have savoured the fragrance and taste of curry ever since I was a small child. It was quite a surprise to me when I discovered that curry is based on Indian and not Chinese inventiveness. Here is a vegetable soup which is raised by its seasonings above the ordinary into something rather special; it is the curry which dominates (without suffocating) the other flavours.

100 g (4 oz) carrots
100 g (4 oz) courgettes
100 g (4 oz) potatoes
100 g (4 oz) Chinese long beans,
runner or French beans, trimmed
100 g (4 oz) Chinese leaves
2 tablespoons oil, preferably
groundnut
2 tablespoons finely chopped
garlic

2 tablespoons finely chopped fresh lemon grass
50 g (2 oz) onions, finely chopped
2 teaspoons turmeric
2 tablespoons curry paste
900 ml (1½ pints) vegetable stock
450 ml (15 fl oz) fresh or tinned coconut milk (see p.14)
1 tablespoon salt

Peel and cut the carrots into 2.5 cm (1 in) rounds. Slice the courgettes into rounds 5 mm (¼ in) thick, or roll cut them (see p.33). Peel and cut the potatoes into 2.5 cm (1 in) cubes. Trim and cut the beans into 7.5 cm (3 in) lengths. Cut the Chinese leaves into 2.5 cm (1 in) pieces.

Heat the oil in a large pan until hot. Add the garlic, lemon grass and onions and cook for about 2 minutes. Stir in the turmeric and curry paste and continue to cook for another 2 minutes. Add the vegetables, stock, coconut milk and salt. Simmer for 8 minutes or until the vegetables are cooked through.

CREAMY AUBERGINE AND TOMATO SOUP
Serves 4–6

This soup is of Indonesian origin. Aubergines are a popular vegetable throughout Southeast Asia. 'Eggplant', as they are called in the USA, derive from the white-skinned egg-shaped variety common in India. In this recipe, tomatoes (a relatively recent addition) are combined with coconut milk (a traditional ingredient) in a vegetable stock to create a nutritious soup that is hearty without being heavy.

350 g (12 oz) aubergine
225 g (8 oz) fresh or tinned tomatoes
100 g (4 oz) onions
1 fresh chilli, seeded
900 ml (1½ pints) vegetable stock
450 ml (15 fl oz) fresh or tinned coconut milk (see p.14)

- *2 tablespoons oil, preferably groundnut*
- *2 tablespoons finely chopped garlic*
- *2 teaspoons sugar*
- *2 teaspoons salt or to taste*
- *½ teaspoon freshly ground white pepper*

Peel and cut the aubergine into 1 cm (½ in) cubes. If you are using fresh tomatoes, peel, seed and cut them into 2.5 cm (1 in) cubes. If you are using tinned tomatoes, cut them into small chunks. Finely chop the onion and chilli.

Bring the stock and coconut milk to simmering point in a large pan. While simmering, heat a wok or large frying-pan and add the oil. When hot, put in the onion, garlic, chilli and aubergine and stir-fry over high heat for about 4 minutes until nicely browned. Drain on kitchen paper, then add to the soup. Add the rest of the ingredients and simmer for 5 minutes.

CHAPTER THREE

COLD DISHES
AND
SALADS

Many oriental dishes contain spices and flavourings that make them delicious, whether they are served hot or cold. Coldness tends to blunt the taste of spices and seasonings, so you can use more of them in cold dishes. In China, there is a lively tradition of serving intricately designed cold food platters at banquets and other special occasions. This is no accident. When food is to be served cold, it is naturally prepared well ahead of time, making it perfect for large gatherings and buffets and, in our day, for picnics. Cold dishes also make warm weather dining more agreeable and pleasant.

Raw vegetable salads are almost unknown in Asia. There, food is always cooked at least a little before it is deemed ready for a sauce or dressing. There are several reasons for this, most notably reasons of hygiene. Brief cooking destroys any bacteria or tiny insects in the vegetables that could be harmful. In societies without a supply of clean water, the eating of raw foods is often unwise; warm weather and no refrigeration contribute to the rapid growth of bacteria. Quick cooking renders food both safe and more easily digestible.

· PEPPERY AUBERGINES ·

Serves 4

India and the Far East consume the greatest quantities of aubergines. This is to be expected as, although this splendid vegetable is now cultivated in warm climates throughout the world, its homeland is India. It has been a traditional food in Eastern cookery for many centuries. This recipe was inspired by my good friend Hwang San in his delightful Hunan-style restaurant, Dong Ting, in Houston, Texas. He steams the aubergines, but I find roasting them just as easy with the same results. Aubergines have a very spongy texture and can absorb a great deal of oil when they are fried or even stir-fried.

This dish works well as a starter. The cooked aubergine is not too filling and the peppercorn sauce stimulates the palate. Because this dish may be made well ahead of time, it is quite practical for entertaining. It is an excellent picnic dish too.

450 g (1 lb) aubergines

Sauce
1½ teaspoons Sichuan peppercorns, roasted and ground (see p.24)
1½ teaspoons salt
1 teaspoon sugar

- *2 tablespoons sesame oil*
- *6 tablespoons finely chopped spring onion tops*
- *2 teaspoons finely chopped fresh coriander*
- *1 tablespoon Chinese white rice vinegar or cider vinegar*

Pre-heat the oven to 200°C/400°F/Gas 6. If you are using Chinese aubergines, roast in the oven for 20 minutes; if you are using the large aubergines, roast for about 30–40 minutes or until they are soft to the touch and cooked through. Allow the aubergines to cool, then peel them. Shred or cut the aubergine flesh into strips.

Arrange the aubergine on a platter. Combine the sauce ingredients, pour over the aubergine and serve at once.

· HOT AND SOUR CUCUMBER SALAD ·
Serves 4

In Thailand, the cucumbers are shorter and thicker than the Western variety. They are also fairly bursting with seeds. But no matter, for whatever type we use, the cucumber's mild flavour and juicy crunchiness come through. In this recipe, the cucumbers are marinated in a piquant vinegary dressing, making them an ideal accompaniment to any fried or grilled dishes. They may also be served as a salad in their own right. By all means experiment: you may find you enjoy an even spicier version. Just add more chillies and garlic.

450 g (1 lb) cucumbers	■	*1 teaspoon salt*
50 ml (2 fl oz) white rice vinegar or cider vinegar	■ ■	*15 g (½ oz) fresh red chilli, finely sliced*
1 tablespoon sugar	■	*1 teaspoon finely chopped garlic*

Slice the cucumbers in half lengthways and, using a teaspoon, remove the seeds. Cut the cucumber halves into 7.5 × 1 cm (3 × ½ in) pieces.

Combine the cucumber pieces with the rest of the ingredients in a bowl and leave to stand for at least 4 hours or more in the fridge, stirring from time to time. When you are ready to serve, drain the cucumber thoroughly.

SESAME-DRESSED SPINACH SALAD

Serves 2–4

Spinach is used extensively in Japanese, Chinese and Indonesian cooking. I have often enjoyed this spinach salad in Japanese restaurants in Southeast Asia, and I was pleased to learn how simple it is to make. In Japan, spinach is picked when it is still quite a small plant; this assures a sweet and tender leaf. The essential technique is to blanch the spinach quickly, plunge it into cold water (to stop the cooking and to preserve the deep colour) and to squeeze out all excess liquid. The spinach is then ready to absorb the flavours of the marinade.

750 g (1½ lb) fresh spinach
1 teaspoon toasted sesame seeds
(see p.24)

Dressing
½ teaspoon salt
1½ tablespoons light soy sauce

2 teaspoons sugar
2 teaspoons Chinese white rice vinegar or cider vinegar
1 tablespoon oil, preferably groundnut

Wash the spinach thoroughly and remove the stalks. Blanch the leaves in a pan of boiling salted water for about 30 seconds. Drain and immerse the leaves in cold water. Drain in a colander. Put the spinach inside a clean linen tea towel and squeeze out all the excess liquid.

Combine all the dressing ingredients in a small bowl and mix thoroughly. Combine the spinach and dressing and leave the salad to marinate in the dressing for at least 1½ hours before serving, or chill and serve within 3 hours. Sprinkle the toasted sesame seeds on top just before serving.

· GREEN AND WHITE JADE SALAD ·

Serves 2–4

This colourful broccoli and cauliflower salad makes a fine starter or picnic dish. The well-flavoured dressing is equally delicious with other vegetable combinations, such as carrots and Brussels sprouts.

225 g (8 oz) broccoli
225 g (8 oz) cauliflower

Dressing
2 tablespoons sesame paste or peanut butter
1 tablespoon Chinese white rice vinegar or cider vinegar

- *1 teaspoon chilli oil*
- *1 teaspoon sesame oil*
- *1 tablespoon light soy sauce*
- *1 teaspoon salt*
- *2 teaspoons sugar*

Cut off the broccoli heads and break them into small florets. Peel the broccoli stalks if necessary and slice. Cut the cauliflower into small florets, about 2.5–3.5 cm (1–1½ in) wide. Blanch the broccoli heads, stalks and cauliflower in a large pan of boiling salted water for 4 minutes. Plunge them into cold water, then drain. Dry the broccoli and cauliflower in a colander or salad spinner and arrange on a platter.

Mix the dressing ingredients together in a bowl or a blender. (This can be done in advance and kept chilled as the sauce should be cold.) Pour the dressing over the vegetables and serve.

EAST-WEST SHREDDED SALAD

Serves 2–4

Raw or almost raw vegetables are enjoyed in most countries, both East and West, but not in Asia, and particularly not in China where they are usually at least stir-fried, blanched or pickled. I enjoy raw vegetables, thus showing my Western culinary influences, but I understand the Chinese preference also. Hence, this East–West compromise: delicious, fresh raw vegetables covered with a heated zesty Chinese-inspired sauce that coats the salad. The result pleases both eye and palate, and creates a refreshing salad for any meal.

100 g (4 oz) carrots
25 g (1 oz) fresh chillies (optional)
4 spring onions
225 g (8 oz) iceberg lettuce
50 g (2 oz) bean sprouts

Dressing
1 tablespoon finely chopped fresh ginger
2 dried chillies, chopped

3 tablespoons finely chopped spring onions
½ teaspoon Sichuan peppercorns, roasted and ground (see p.24)
1 tablespoon light soy sauce
1 tablespoon Chinese white rice vinegar or cider vinegar
2 tablespoons oil, preferably groundnut
2 teaspoons sesame oil

Peel and cut the carrots into 5 cm (2 in) fine shreds. Cut the chillies, spring onions and lettuce into 5 cm (2 in) fine shreds. In a large bowl, mix all the vegetables together.

Combine all the dressing ingredients, except the oils, in a heatproof bowl. Heat the oil in a small saucepan or wok until almost smoking. Pour the hot oils over the dressing ingredients and allow to cool for 5 minutes. Pour the dressing over the vegetables and toss thoroughly. Serve at once.

· S P I N A C H   I N   S O Y   S A U C E ·
Serves 2–4

Spinach is a nutritious vegetable with a fine flavour. The trend throughout the West is of consuming more and more fresh spinach instead of tinned or frozen, and raw spinach leaves are increasingly used in salad. This recipe is based on a traditional southern Chinese method but, instead of serving the cooked spinach warm, I serve it cold. In the area around Canton there is a variety called water spinach, which has a milder taste and which, when cooked, presents a pleasing contrast between the crunchy stalk and soft leaves. It may sometimes be found in Chinese grocers and I encourage you to look for it to try, but ordinary fresh spinach will do very well.

750 g (1½ lb) fresh spinach

Sauce
1½ tablespoons dark soy sauce

2 teaspoons sesame oil
2 teaspoons sugar

Remove the stalks from the spinach and wash the leaves well. Blanch the leaves for a few seconds in a pan of boiling water until just wilted. Remove and freshen them in cold water to prevent further cooking. Drain the leaves in a colander, then place on a linen tea towel and squeeze out all the excess liquid. Arrange on a serving dish.

Mix the sauce ingredients together and pour over the spinach. This dish can remain at room temperature until ready to serve.

· CHINESE AUBERGINE SALAD ·

Serves 4

This is a tasty salad with a piquant dressing. Roasting the aubergines preserves their moist, sweet flavour. Quickly made, this dish can be served warm or cold.

450 g (1 lb) aubergines

Dressing
2 tablespoons finely chopped spring onions

- *2 teaspoons chilli oil*
- *1½ tablespoons light soy sauce*
- *1 teaspoon finely chopped garlic*

Pre-heat the oven to 200°C/400°F/Gas 6. If you are using Chinese aubergines, roast in the oven for 20 minutes; if you are using the large aubergines, roast for about 30–40 minutes or until they are soft and cooked through. Allow to cool, then peel. Cut the aubergine flesh into strips.

Arrange the aubergine on a platter. Combine the dressing ingredients and pour over the aubergine. Serve the salad immediately or chill and serve the next day.

· COLD GREEN BEAN SALAD ·
Serves 2–4

Simplicity itself, this recipe takes a favourite vegetable and gives it a touch of Southeast Asian zest. Serve these beans either as a salad or as a side vegetable dish. They may be prepared well ahead of time.

225 g (8 oz) Chinese long beans,
runner or French beans, trimmed
1 tablespoon oil, preferably
groundnut
1 small onion, finely chopped

Dressing
1 tablespoon light soy sauce

2 teaspoons toasted sesame seeds
(see p.24)
2 tablespoons lemon juice
2 teaspoons sesame oil
1 teaspoon salt
2 teaspoons chilli oil

If you are using Chinese long beans or runner beans, cut them into 7.5 cm (3 in) lengths. If you are using French beans, leave whole. Blanch the beans in a large pan of boiling salted water for 2 minutes. Immerse them in cold water, drain thoroughly and set aside.

Heat a wok or frying-pan and add the oil. When moderately hot, add the onion and stir-fry for 2 minutes, then allow to cool. Add to the beans.

Combine all the dressing ingredients and toss with the beans and onion. Serve the salad immediately or chill and serve the next day.

· BEAN SPROUT SALAD ·
Serves 4

Bean sprouts have been enjoyed in China and Southeast Asia for centuries but have only been introduced to the West in the last twenty years or so. They are essentially a transitional food, as it were, midway between the seed or bean from which they spring and the vegetable they will become. They have significant nutritional value, a nutty flavour and crisp texture as well. Mung beans and soya beans are the favoured sprouts among the Chinese, who love them cooked but never in raw form. Lightly blanched, as in this recipe, the sprouts lose their raw taste but retain their crispness and flavour.

450 g (1 lb) fresh bean sprouts
1 fresh red chilli, seeded and finely shredded

Dressing
1½ tablespoons light soy sauce
1 teaspoon oil, preferably groundnut
2 teaspoons sesame oil

1 teaspoon chilli oil
1 teaspoon finely chopped garlic
2 tablespoons finely chopped spring onions
½ teaspoon sugar
½ teaspoon salt
¼ teaspoon freshly ground white pepper

Trim and discard both ends of the bean sprouts. Blanch the bean sprouts in a large pan of boiling water for 1 minute. Drain in a colander, immerse them in cold water, then drain again.

Combine the dressing ingredients in a small bowl. Mix the dressing together with the bean sprouts and chilli.

ASPARAGUS WITH TANGY MUSTARD DRESSING
Serves 2–4

Asparagus is a relative newcomer to the cast of vegetables in oriental cuisine, but there is no doubt it has won a permanent starring role in the repertoire. Its popularity is based on contrasts: properly cooked, it has a firm but soft texture, a delicate yet earthy, assertive flavour – and a brilliant colour. In this Japanese-style recipe, the asparagus is simply cooked by quickly blanching, the briefest processing possible. The mustard-ginger dressing only highlights and never intrudes upon the taste of the asparagus. Since asparagus is relatively expensive, indulge yourself and savour this recipe when it is in season. Serve it as a starter or side dish for a special meal.

450 g (1 lb) fresh asparagus

Dressing
1 teaspoon dried mustard
1 teaspoon hot water

1 egg yolk
1 tablespoon dark soy sauce
1 teaspoon finely chopped fresh ginger
¼ teaspoon salt

Break off the woody ends of the asparagus and cut the stalks into 7.5 cm (3 in) diagonal pieces. Blanch the asparagus in a large pan of boiling salted water for 2 minutes. Plunge them into cold water, then drain in a colander. Pat dry with kitchen paper.

In a small bowl, mix the mustard and hot water together and stir until it becomes a thick paste. Add the rest of the dressing ingredients and mix well.

Arrange the asparagus on a serving platter and pour the dressing over. Serve immediately or within 3 hours.

· CRISPY NOODLE SALAD ·
Serves 4

I first enjoyed this salad, called Mee Krob, in a rather unpretentious restaurant in Bangkok. There are a number of different variations on the crispy noodle salad theme, with many people preferring a sweet and sour salad. At home, I set out to recreate the combination of textures, flavours and colours that had most impressed me in Thailand, and this recipe is my favourite – a beautifully arranged salad platter that is dressed and tossed at the last minute. Such a salad is ideal as a starter for any meal.

300 ml (10 fl oz) oil, preferably groundnut, for deep-frying
100 g (4 oz) rice noodles, rice vermicelli or rice sticks

Sauce
2 garlic cloves, crushed
2 tablespoons finely chopped shallots
3 tablespoons light soy sauce
1 tablespoon sugar
2 tablespoons Chinese white vinegar or cider vinegar

Garnish
100 g (4 oz) beancurd
100 g (4 oz) bean sprouts
3 spring onions, shredded
1 fresh chilli, shredded
fresh coriander sprigs

Heat the oil in a deep-fat fryer or wok until moderately hot. Deep-fry the noodles until crispy and puffed up. Remove from the oil with a slotted spoon and drain on kitchen paper. You may have to do this in several batches. (Leave the oil in the deep-fat fryer or wok as you will need it for the beancurd.)

Cut the beancurd into 1 cm (½ in) cubes. Re-heat the oil until very hot and deep-fry the beancurd cubes until golden. Remove with a slotted spoon and drain on kitchen paper.

Combine the sauce ingredients in a small bowl and mix well.

Place the crispy noodles on a serving platter and garnish attractively with the beancurd, bean sprouts, spring onions, chilli and coriander. Pour the dressing over the salad just before serving and mix well.

CHAPTER FOUR

VEGETABLE DISHES

Vegetables are important in any cuisine that is nutritious, flavourful and colourful. In the Cantonese cuisine of south China, considered among the most nutritious in the world, more vegetables of diverse texture, shape, size and colour are used than in almost any other culinary tradition. My mother, who is of Cantonese origin, consequently relied heavily on vegetables in our home cooking. She used traditional Chinese vegetables whenever they were available, but she reached out to harvest the Western cornucopia as well. In Chinese cookery, technique is more important even than the ingredients. My mother took standard European vegetables and prepared them so well that, unlike my Western schoolmates, I loved to eat them. As my mother cooked them, the vegetables retained their fresh flavours, textures, nutritious vitamins and colours.

Many vegetables have delicate textures; most have only subtle flavours. How does one cook them and yet preserve their qualities? Well, practice makes perfect, especially to avoid overcooking. With vegetables, you need to nibble, taste, nibble, taste as you cook.

rinse the beans again under warm running water until the water runs clear. Dampen the muslin and spread one piece over the tin lid, pan or steamer. Spread the beans over the cloth and sprinkle them with more lukewarm water. Cover the beans with the second piece of muslin and then put them in a warm, dark place. Keep them moist by sprinkling with water several times over the next few days. In three days you should have white crisp sprouts.

BITTER MELON

Used as a vegetable, bitter melon has a strong flavour worthy of its name. The greener the melon, the more bitter its taste, so many cooks look for the milder yellow-green skinned melon. To use, cut in half, seed and discard the interior membrane. To lessen the bitter taste, either blanch or salt according to the instructions in the recipe.

CHINESE BROCCOLI

Chinese broccoli or gai lan (*Brassica oleracea capitata*) does not taste like European broccoli (calabrese). It is very crunchy, slightly bitter and resembles Swiss chard in flavour. It has deep olive green leaves and sometimes has white flowers. Chinese broccoli is usually only available at Chinese grocers. If you can find it, look for firm stalks and leaves which look fresh and green. It is prepared in exactly the same way as broccoli, and should be stored in a plastic bag in the vegetable compartment of the fridge where it will keep for several days. If you cannot find Chinese broccoli, substitute ordinary broccoli instead.

CHINESE CHIVES

Chinese chives are related to common chives, but their taste is much stronger and garlic-like, and their flowers can be used as well as the blades. Chinese chives can be found in Chinese markets but are also very easy to grow in home herb gardens. Look for wide flat blades and sprays of white, star-shaped flowers. They can be substituted for ordinary chives, but adjust the quantity to allow for their stronger flavour. Rinse and dry the chives, store them in a plastic bag in the fridge and use as soon as possible.

Chinese Flowering Cabbage

Chinese flowering cabbage (*Brassica rapa*) is usually known by its more familiar Cantonese name, choi sam. It has yellowish green leaves and may have small yellow flowers which are eaten along with the leaves and stalks. It is obtainable from Chinese grocers and is delicious stir-fried.

Chinese Greens

Chinese greens (*Brassica chinensis*) is an attractive vegetable with a long, smooth, milky-white stalk and large, crinkly, dark green leaves. It is similar to Swiss chard, and has been grown for centuries in China, where it is known as bok choy. In the West, it is sometimes called Chinese white cabbage or Chinese chard, and it has a light fresh taste and requires little cooking. It is usually available from Chinese grocers. Swiss chard or spinach can be substituted if you cannot obtain Chinese greens.

Chinese Leaves

Chinese leaves (*Brassica pekinensis*) look rather like a large, tightly packed cos lettuce with firm, pale green, crinkled leaves. It is sometimes known as Chinese or Peking cabbage, and is widely available in greengrocers, supermarkets and Chinese grocers. It is a delicious crunchy vegetable with a mild but distinctive taste. If you cannot find it, use English white cabbage instead.

Chinese Long Beans

Also known as yard-long beans. Chinese long beans (*Vigna sesquipedalis*) can grow to about 1 metre (3 feet) in length. Although runner beans and French beans can be substituted for the long beans, they are not related, the long beans having originated in Asia. Buy beans that are fresh and bright green, with no dark marks. You will usually find beans sold in looped bunches. Store the beans in a plastic bag in the fridge and use within four days.

Chinese White Radish (Mooli)

Chinese white radish is sometimes known in Britain as mooli. It is long and white and rather like a carrot in shape but usually very much larger. A winter radish or root, it can withstand long cooking without disintegrating, so it absorbs the flavour of a sauce yet retains its distinctive radish taste and texture. It must be peeled before use. Chinese white radish can be bought in many supermarkets and greengrocers and in oriental and Chinese grocers. They should be firm, heavy and unblemished, slightly translucent inside and not tough and fibrous. Store in a plastic bag in the vegetable compartment of the fridge where they will keep for over a week. If you cannot find white radish, use turnips instead.

MANGETOUT

These tender flat green pods combine a crisp texture with a sweet, fresh flavour. Mangetout are delicious whether simply stir-fried with a little oil and salt, or combined with other ingredients. Shredded, they add a crisp texture and sweet taste to stuffings and other dishes. They produce a unique crunchy salad when blanched and tossed in a dressing. Before cooking, the ends should be trimmed. Mangetout are available from greengrocers and supermarkets. Look for pods that are firm with very small peas, which means they will be tender and young. They keep for at least a week in the vegetable compartment of the fridge.

SHALLOTS

Shallots are mild-flavoured members of the onion family. They are small – about the size of pickling onions – with copper-red skins and a distinctive onion taste. However, they are not as strong or overpowering as ordinary onions. I think they are an excellent substitute for Chinese onions, which are unobtainable in the West. They are expensive, but a few go a long way. Buy them at good greengrocers, supermarkets and delicatessens. Keep them in a cool, dry place (but not the fridge) and peel them as you would an onion. If you cannot find shallots, use pickling onions or spring onions.

SPINACH

European varieties of spinach are quite different from those used in China, although they make satisfactory substitutes for the Asian variety. Spinach is most commonly stir-fried, so frozen spinach is obviously unsuitable. Chinese water spinach (*Ipomoea aquatica*) is available in some greengrocers and in Chinese grocers. It has hollow stalks and delicate, pointed green leaves, lighter in colour than common spinach and with a milder taste. Cook when very fresh, preferably on the day it is bought.

WATERCHESTNUTS

Sweet, crisp, white waterchestnuts have been eaten in China for centuries as a snack, having first been boiled in their skins or peeled and simmered in rock sugar. In cooked dishes they are especially popular in the south, where they are sometimes grown between rice plants in paddies. (This is why they are often muddy.) They are not part of the chestnut family at all, but an edible root or bulb about the size of a walnut that forms at the base of the stem. Tinned waterchestnuts are a pale version of the fresh ones, because both the crispness and the flavour are lost in the canning process. Fresh waterchestnuts can sometimes be obtained from Chinese grocers or good supermarkets and will keep unpeeled in a paper bag in the fridge for up to 2 weeks. Look for a firm, hard texture. The skin should be tight and taut, not wrinkled. If they are mushy, they are too old; feel them all over for soft, rotten spots. If you peel waterchestnuts in advance, cover with cold water to prevent browning and store in the fridge. If you cannot find fresh waterchestnuts, tinned ones are sold in many supermarkets and Chinese grocers. Rinse well in cold water before using, and store any unused ones in the fridge in a jar of water. They will keep for several weeks if you change the water daily.

· SUMMER PEPPER STIR-FRY ·
Serves 2–4

Here is an ensemble of colours, flavours, tastes and textures that will appeal to the eye as well as the palate.

25 g (1 oz) Chinese dried
mushrooms
2 eggs, beaten
3 teaspoons sesame oil
¼ teaspoon salt
5 teaspoons oil, preferably
groundnut
1 tablespoon finely chopped spring
onions
1 tablespoon finely chopped fresh
ginger
1 tablespoon finely chopped garlic
1 small fresh chilli, seeded and
finely shredded

225 g (8 oz) red, yellow or green
peppers (about 1 each)
2 teaspoons rice wine or dry
sherry
1 teaspoon light soy sauce
1 teaspoon sugar
salt and freshly ground black
pepper to taste
100 g (4 oz) bean sprouts,
preferably trimmed at both ends

Garnish
2 tablespoons finely chopped
spring onions

Soak the dried mushrooms in warm water for 20 minutes or until soft. Squeeze out the excess water and cut away the stalks. Shred the mushroom caps and set aside.

Combine the beaten eggs with 1 teaspoon of sesame oil and the salt in a small bowl. Heat a frying-pan or wok over moderate heat and add 2 teaspoons of the groundnut oil. Add the egg-mixture and spread over the surface of the pan until it forms a thin crêpe-like pancake. Remove from the heat and, when cool, cut the egg pancake into thin shreds and set aside.

Heat a wok or large frying-pan over high heat and add the remaining groundnut oil. Put in the spring onions, ginger, garlic and chilli and stir-fry for 30 seconds. Add the peppers, mushrooms, rice wine, soy sauce, sugar, salt and pepper. Stir-fry for 2 minutes until the peppers are soft. Stir in the bean sprouts and egg shreds and stir-fry gently for another 2 minutes, then add 2 teaspoons of sesame oil. Remove the mixture to a serving platter and garnish with the spring onions. Serve at once.

RAINBOW VEGETABLES IN LETTUCE CUPS

Serves 4–6

This is a version of a popular Hong Kong dish that usually includes minced lean beef, pigeon or pork. But the texture of the meat or poultry is not missed when one savours the tasty crunchiness of the vegetables combined with crispy fried bean thread noodles, cupped in a refreshing lettuce leaf and flavoured with hoisin sauce. This dish makes a good starter for a festive meal, as guests can fill their own lettuce cups at the table.

450 g (1 lb) iceberg lettuce
100 g (4 oz) carrots
225 g (8 oz) courgettes
100 g (4 oz) red peppers
100 g (4 oz) yellow peppers
300 ml (10 fl oz) oil, preferably groundnut, for deep-frying
25 g (1 oz) bean thread (transparent) noodles
3 tablespoons coarsely chopped garlic

½ teaspoon salt
2 tablespoons rice wine or dry sherry
3 tablespoons vegetable stock
100 g (4 oz) fresh or tinned waterchestnuts, coarsely chopped
2 teaspoons light soy sauce
1½ tablespoons dark soy sauce
3 tablespoons hoisin sauce

Separate, wash and dry the lettuce leaves. Finely dice the carrots, courgettes and peppers.

In a deep-fat fryer or large wok, heat the oil until almost smoking. Turn off the heat and deep-fry the noodles until they are crisp and puffed up. Drain on kitchen paper.

Heat a wok or large frying-pan and add 1 tablespoon of the oil in which you have fried the noodles. Put in the garlic, salt, carrots, rice wine and stock and stir-fry for about 2 minutes. Then add the rest of the vegetables (except the lettuce) and waterchestnuts together with the soy sauces and stir-fry for 3–4 minutes. Turn the mixture onto a platter. Arrange the lettuce and noodles on separate platters, put the hoisin sauce in a small bowl, and serve.

STIR-FRIED 'SILVER SPROUTS'

Serves 4

Small mung beans provide these sprouts. In Hong Kong, markets sell fresh bean sprouts plucked or trimmed at both ends. In that form they have a clean, fresh look and are ready to use, but the trimming process takes some time. They are a very nutritious addition to salads and stir-fried dishes, their mild flavour and crunchiness providing a delightful touch to every meal. When they are stir-fried with beancurd and other ingredients, as here, their colour appears as a shimmering silver, hence the name of this recipe.

Try to obtain pressed seasoned beancurd. It is cooked in a soy-flavoured sauce which also imparts a pleasant brownish colour to it. If unavailable, you may substitute fresh firm beancurd, but you must weight it down with a heavy lid for at least 2 hours to make it even firmer and less moist. It will also have less flavour, so remember to increase your seasonings. Pan-fry the beancurd until it is firm before stir-frying, otherwise it may fall apart; this will affect the appearance but not the taste.

25 g (1 oz) Chinese dried mushrooms	1 ½ teaspoons salt
225 g (8 oz) bean sprouts	¼ teaspoon freshly ground black pepper
225 g (8 oz) pressed seasoned beancurd	1 tablespoon oil, preferably groundnut
50 g (2 oz) celery	2 teaspoons chilli oil
100 g (4 oz) green peppers	2 tablespoons rice wine or dry sherry
50 g (2 oz) carrots	3–4 tablespoons water
4 spring onions	

Soak the mushrooms in a large bowl of warm water for 20 minutes. Drain them and squeeze out any excess liquid. Discard the tough stalks, finely shred the caps and put them aside.

Trim the bean sprouts. Cut the pressed beancurd, celery, peppers, carrots and spring onions into fine shreds.

Heat a wok or large frying-pan over moderate heat and add the oils. Put in the salt, pepper and carrots and stir-fry for 1 minute. Add the celery, mushrooms, beancurd, peppers and spring onions and continue to stir-fry for 2 minutes. Stir in the rice wine and water and stir-fry until most of the liquid has evaporated. Turn onto a plate and serve.

DRY-BRAISED BAMBOO SHOOTS WITH BROCCOLI

Serves 4

Fresh bamboo shoots are rare outside the Southeast Asian sub-tropics, where they feature in many recipes as a vegetable, as part of a stuffing or as a garnish for many dishes. They are boiled before eating because they contain a cyanide-type poison which must be broken down. I have often wondered how it was discovered that so dangerous a food could be transformed into a delicacy – who first dared to try fresh bamboo shoots? However, those of us outside Southeast Asia must make do with the tinned variety. This is unfortunate, because fresh bamboo shoots are a true delicacy. The tinned version is an acceptable substitute but one that requires a little work to restore the flavour lost in the canning process. Served with rice, this recipe makes a light and very appetizing vegetarian meal.

225 g (8 oz) fresh broccoli
550 g (1 ¼ lb) tinned bamboo shoots
150 ml (5 fl oz) oil, preferably groundnut
1 teaspoon finely chopped fresh ginger
1 teaspoon salt

- 1 tablespoon yellow bean sauce
- 1 tablespoon sugar
- 3 tablespoons rice wine or dry sherry
- 150 ml (5 fl oz) vegetable stock
- 1 tablespoon oil, preferably groundnut
- 2 teaspoons finely chopped garlic

Separate the broccoli heads into florets, then peel the stalks if necessary and slice. Blanch the broccoli pieces in a large pan of boiling salted water for several minutes. Drain and immerse them in cold water. Drain again thoroughly in a colander and set aside. Rinse the tinned bamboo shoots well.

Cut the bamboo shoots into 7.5 × 1 cm (3 × ½ in) pieces and dry thoroughly with kitchen paper. Heat the 150 ml (5 fl oz) of oil in a wok or large frying-pan. Pan-fry the bamboo shoots until they are nicely brown. Drain thoroughly on kitchen paper and set aside.

Pour off all but 1 tablespoon of the oil and re-heat the wok. Add the ginger, ½ teaspoon of the salt and the bean sauce, and stir-fry for 1 minute. Return the bamboo shoots to the wok and add the sugar, rice wine and stock. Braise for 3–5 minutes over high heat until most of the liquid has evaporated. Remove and set aside.

Wipe the wok clean, re-heat and add the 1 tablespoon of fresh oil. When smoking slightly, add the garlic, remaining salt and broccoli to the wok and stir-fry for 1 minute. Return the bamboo shoots to the wok and continue to stir-fry for another 2–3 minutes or until heated through. Turn the mixture onto a platter and serve at once.

· MOCK VEGETABLE PASTA ·
Serves 4

In Chinese vegetarian cookery, a dish is not always what it appears to be. For example, 'mock duck' is taro root stuffed with minced vegetables and fried to a golden brown to look like duck. I enjoy the fun and imaginativeness of such creativity and here I take courgettes and cut them into long thin strips to look like pasta. I then salt them to remove excess moisture and, in the process, firm their texture. Quickly stir-fried with traditional Chinese seasonings, the resulting dish looks and tastes like pasta – my guests are always surprised by its lightness, flavour and texture. Do not overcook the courgettes – they should have a firmness to the bite. This mock pasta is delicious cold, and it can also function as a vegetable or salad serving: it is perfect for picnics too.

900 g (2 lb) courgettes
1 tablespoon salt
1 tablespoon oil, preferably groundnut
1 tablespoon finely chopped garlic

- *2 teaspoons finely chopped fresh ginger*
- *2 tablespoons finely chopped fresh coriander*
- *2 tablespoons finely chopped spring onions, green parts only*

OPPOSITE: **Peppery Aubergines** *(page 82)*

COSY AUTUMN SUPPER
Sesame-Dressed Spinach Salad *(page 84)*
Savoury Beancurd Casserole *(page 139)*
Long-Grain Rice *(page 186)*
Sweet Wontons *(page 204)*

Cut the courgettes into long thin strips resembling pasta. Put the strips into a colander and sprinkle with the salt. Leave to stand for 20 minutes. Then wrap the courgettes in a linen tea towel and squeeze out the excess liquid.

Heat a wok or large frying-pan over moderate heat and add the oil. Put in the garlic and ginger and stir-fry for 30 seconds. Add the courgettes, fresh coriander and spring onions and continue to stir-fry for 4 minutes or until the courgettes are heated through. Turn the mixture onto a platter and serve warm or at room temperature.

STIR-FRIED ASPARAGUS IN BLACK BEAN SAUCE

Serves 2

Asparagus is expensive even when in season, but it is so exquisite a treat it is worth buying as often as you can. Not a traditional ingredient of Southeast Asian cuisines, it has been very quickly incorporated during this century. It goes well with this pungent and robust black bean sauce, a traditional Chinese seasoning. With rice and another light dish, this recipe forms a complete meal for two.

450 g (1 lb) fresh asparagus	2 teaspoons chilli bean sauce
1 tablespoon oil, preferably groundnut	150 ml (5 fl oz) vegetable stock
2 teaspoons finely chopped fresh ginger	1 teaspoon sugar
2 teaspoons finely chopped garlic	3 tablespoons rice wine or dry sherry
2 tablespoons black beans, coarsely chopped	1 teaspoon sesame oil

Cut the asparagus diagonally into 7.5 cm (3 in) lengths.

Heat a wok or large frying-pan and add the oil. When hot, add the ginger, garlic and black beans and stir-fry for a few seconds. Add the chilli bean sauce and, a few seconds later, add the asparagus and stir-

OPPOSITE: **Summer Pepper Stir-Fry** *(page 100)*

fry for 2 minutes. Stir in the stock, sugar and rice wine. Cook the mixture over high heat for about 2 minutes, stirring continuously. Add the sesame oil, give the mixture a couple of stirs, and serve at once.

BUTTON MUSHROOMS IN SOY SAUCE

Serves 2–4

Button mushrooms are unknown in the East, but I have found that they, like all good edible fungi, are perfectly amenable to Chinese and other Southeast Asian spices and seasoning.

2 teaspoons oil, preferably groundnut
2 garlic cloves, crushed
450 g (1 lb) small whole button mushrooms

2 tablespoons dark soy sauce
1 teaspoon sugar
2 tablespoons rice wine or dry sherry

Heat a wok or large frying-pan and add the oil. Put in the garlic and stir-fry for 30 seconds. Add the mushrooms and stir-fry for 1 minute. Stir in the soy sauce, sugar and rice wine. Turn the heat down and simmer slowly for 5 minutes, stirring from time to time. When the mushrooms are cooked, turn the heat back to high and continue stirring until most of the liquid has evaporated and the dish is ready to be served.

MU-SHU VEGETABLES WITH CHINESE PANCAKES

Serves 4

This is a vegetarian version of a traditional Chinese favourite, Mu-Shu Pork. Here, I rely upon an unusually flavourful combination of spices, vegetables and condiments. Particularly important to this recipe are the Chinese dried wood ears and lily buds. These may be difficult to obtain but are worth the extra effort of searching for them.

Their textures and the flavours they absorb in the stir-frying are the basis for the success of the dish. When the combined ingredients are eaten with Chinese Pancakes (see p.41) and hoisin sauce, what might be an ordinary dish is transformed into a festive affair. Most of the preparation may be done ahead of time and, once the pancakes are made, the rest is easily accomplished, making this a perfect dish for a dinner party. You may experiment with your own seasonal favourite vegetables or serve with rice instead of pancakes.

4 eggs, beaten
4 teaspoons sesame oil
1 teaspoon salt
2 tablespoons oil, preferably groundnut
15 g (½ oz) Chinese dried wood ears
15 g (½ oz) Chinese lily buds
100 g (4 oz) red peppers
4 spring onions

- *3 tablespoons rice wine or dry sherry*
- *1 tablespoon finely chopped garlic*
- *1 tablespoon finely chopped fresh ginger*
- *2 tablespoons dark soy sauce*
- *175 g (6 oz) bean sprouts*
- *Chinese Pancakes (see p.41)*
- *hoisin sauce, for dipping*

Combine the beaten eggs with 2 teaspoons of the sesame oil and the salt in a small bowl. Heat a frying-pan or wok over moderate heat and add 1 tablespoon of the oil. Pour in the egg mixture and spread it quickly over the surface of the pan until it forms a thin crêpe-like pancake. There is no need to turn it over. Remove from the heat and, when cool, shred the egg pancake and set aside.

Soak the dried wood ears and lily buds in warm water for about 20 minutes until soft. Meanwhile, finely shred the peppers and spring onions. Squeeze the excess liquid from the wood ears and lily buds. Finely shred the wood ears and snap off the hard ends of the lily buds.

Heat a wok or large frying-pan over high heat and add the remaining groundnut oil. When almost smoking, add the wood ears, lily buds and rice wine and stir-fry for 1 minute. Add the garlic, ginger and dark soy sauce and stir-fry for another minute. Then put in the shredded egg and bean sprouts and continue to stir-fry for 3 minutes until the ingredients are thoroughly mixed. Stir in the remaining sesame oil and turn onto a large platter. Serve with the Chinese pancakes and hoisin sauce.

VEGETABLE MEDLEY WITH TOMATO-GARLIC SAUCE

Serves 4–6

In oriental cooking, the preference is often for dipping sauces rather than for sauces that cover the food on the plate. In this recipe from Vietnam, each type of vegetable is blanched individually, thus making allowance for the different cooking requirements of each vegetable. Remember to plunge them immediately into cold water to prevent further cooking. The dipping sauce is quite lively, which is exactly what the plain, sweet, cool vegetables need. This is an ideal dish for a buffet and cocktails.

100 g (4 oz) Chinese long beans, runner or French beans, trimmed
100 g (4 oz) courgettes
100 g (4 oz) cauliflower
100 g (4 oz) broccoli
100 g (4 oz) carrots
100 g (4 oz) mangetout, trimmed
1 tablespoon oil, preferably groundnut

Sauce
2 tablespoons finely chopped garlic

3 tablespoons finely chopped shallots
1 teaspoon seeded and finely chopped dried chillies
350 g (12 oz) fresh or tinned tomatoes
1 tablespoon light soy sauce

Garnish
1 tablespoon finely chopped fresh coriander

Cut the beans into 7.5 cm (3 in) lengths. Cut the courgettes into 7.5 × 1 cm (3 × ½ in) pieces. Cut the cauliflower into small florets about 2.5–3.5 cm (1–1½ in) wide. Cut off the broccoli head and break it into small florets. Peel and thinly slice the broccoli stalks. Peel and cut the carrots into 7.5 × 1 cm (3 × ½ in) pieces.

Blanch each of the vegetables separately in a large pan of boiling salted water: 1 minute for the mangetout, 2 minutes for the beans and courgettes, 4 minutes for the cauliflower, broccoli and carrots. As you take out each vegetable, plunge it into cold water until cooled, then drain well.

For the sauce, if you are using fresh tomatoes, skin, seed and cut into 2.5 cm (1 in) cubes. If you are using tinned tomatoes, chop into small chunks. Combine the tomatoes with the rest of the sauce ingredients and purée the mixture in a blender or food processor. Arrange the vegetables on a serving platter together with the dipping sauce in a separate bowl. Garnish the sauce with the fresh coriander. Serve immediately or chill and serve later.

ASPARAGUS WITH CHINESE BLACK MUSHROOMS
Serves 2–4

Asparagus is a vegetable which readily combines with many other foods in the most congenial fashion. Here, it is joined with fleshy, smokey Chinese dried mushrooms, with both vegetables absorbing the essences of each other and of the sauce. I suggest that, if available, you use a larger variety of asparagus. This is a wholesome and satisfying dish, easy to prepare and, with rice, a meal in itself.

450 g (1 lb) large asparagus
25 g (1 oz) Chinese dried mushrooms
1 tablespoon oil, preferably groundnut
2 garlic cloves, lightly crushed

¼ teaspoon salt
150 ml (5 fl oz) vegetable stock
2 tablespoons dark soy sauce
1 teaspoon cornflour mixed with 1 teaspoon cold water

Cut the asparagus diagonally into 5 cm (2 in) lengths, discarding the hard woody ends.

Soak the dried mushrooms in warm water for about 20 minutes. Remove the mushrooms from the water and squeeze out any excess liquid. Cut off the stalks and discard them.

Heat a wok or large frying-pan over moderate heat and add the oil. Put in the garlic, salt and asparagus and stir-fry for 1 minute. Add the stock and mushrooms and continue to stir-fry for 3 minutes or until the asparagus is cooked. Add the soy sauce and blended cornflour and continue to cook until the sauce has been reduced to a glaze. Give the mixture a final stir, turn onto a platter and serve at once.

· VEGETABLE TEMPURA ·
Serves 6–8

Of all deep-fried foods, I prefer Japanese tempura. The delicate coating of batter allows the fresh vegetable flavours to come through; there is crispness without the heaviness generally associated with batter-fried foods. The secret of tempura's lace-like quality lies in the use of a thin batter made with *very* cold or iced water and not mixed together until the very last moment. Although tempura is commonly used with seafood such as prawns, it works as deliciously with vegetables. Cooking the tempura, by dipping the prepared vegetables in the batter and deep-frying them quickly, takes a bit of practice. The tempura must be served immediately. For an authentic Japanese taste, *dashi* would be used in preference to the stock in the dipping sauce.

100 g (4 oz) cauliflower	**Sauce**
100 g (4 oz) courgettes	*50 ml (2 fl oz) vegetable stock*
100 g (4 oz) carrots	*3 tablespoons sake, rice wine or*
100 g (4 oz) aubergines	*dry sherry*
50 g (2 oz) Chinese long beans,	*2 tablespoons light soy sauce*
runner beans or French beans,	*1 tablespoon sugar*
trimmed	
1 small onion	**Batter**
100 g (4 oz) small whole button	*1 egg, beaten*
mushrooms	*150 ml (5 fl oz) very cold water*
600 ml (1 pint) oil, preferably	*100 g (4 oz) plain flour, sifted*
groundnut, for deep-frying	*½ teaspoon baking powder*

Cut the cauliflower into small florets about 3.5 cm (1½ in) wide. Cut the courgettes, carrots and aubergines into thin 10 cm (4 in) long slices. Cut the beans into 10 cm (4 in) lengths. Thinly slice the onion.

In a small pan, simmer the sauce ingredients together for 5 minutes. Remove the sauce from the heat, leave to cool, then pour the sauce into a small serving bowl and set aside.

Combine the batter ingredients together in a bowl and quickly strain through a fine sieve. (Do this just before you are about to deep-fry, while the oil is heating.)

Heat the oil in a deep-fat fryer or large wok until hot. Dip the vegetables in the batter and fry until golden and crispy. Remove with a slotted spoon and drain on kitchen paper. You will have to do this in several batches. Serve immediately with the dipping sauce.

GREEN BEANS IN PUNGENT SAUCE

Serves 2–4

I often enjoyed this easy-to-make homely dish as a child. Fresh green beans are a nutritious and inexpensive vegetable and lend themselves to spices and seasonings that complement their delicate flavour. In this recipe, the pungent spiciness of fermented chilli beancurd turns the vegetable into something quite special. You will find fermented beancurd at Chinese grocers; you may choose from various types, ranging from mild to quite spicy. In using so lively a spice as chilli beancurd, remember that a little goes a long way.

1 tablespoon oil, preferably groundnut
2 garlic cloves, crushed
1 tablespoon fermented chilli beancurd
¼ teaspoon salt

- *450 g (1 lb) Chinese long beans or runner beans, trimmed and sliced, or French beans, trimmed and left whole*
- *3 tablespoons rice wine or dry sherry*
- *2 tablespoons water*

Heat a wok or large frying-pan and add the oil. When moderately hot, add the garlic, beancurd and salt and stir-fry for about 30 seconds. Add the beans, rice wine and water and continue to stir-fry over a moderately high heat for about 5 minutes or until the beans are thoroughly cooked, adding more water if necessary to keep the beans moist. Serve at once.

· SICHUAN FRIED AUBERGINES ·
Serves 4–6

Aubergines are delicious when fried in a light batter, which prevents too much oil penetrating the aubergines. They are then enlivened by what the Chinese call a 'fish flavouring' sauce, a non-fishy mixture of spices and seasonings normally used in the preparation of fish. Both the aubergines and the batter readily absorb the sauce. This sauce is not to be confused with the commercially bottled fish sauce widely used in Southeast Asian cooking. Try to buy Chinese aubergines as they have a more delicate taste; however, ordinary aubergines will suffice. This is an excellent starter. If you serve it with cocktails, serve the sauce separately.

450 g (1 lb) aubergines
450 ml (15 fl oz) oil, preferably groundnut, for deep-frying

Batter
50 g (2 oz) plain flour
150 ml (5 fl oz) water
¼ teaspoon salt

Sauce
1 tablespoon oil, preferably groundnut
3 tablespoons finely chopped spring onions

- 1 tablespoon finely chopped fresh ginger
- 2 teaspoons chilli bean sauce
- 150 ml (5 fl oz) vegetable stock
- 2 tablespoons rice wine or dry sherry
- 1 tablespoon Chinese black rice vinegar or cider vinegar
- 3 tablespoons tomato purée
- 2 teaspoons sugar
- 2 tablespoons dark soy sauce
- 1 teaspoon cornflour mixed with 1 teaspoon water

Cut the aubergines into 3.5 × 7.5 cm (1½ × 3 in) slices. Do not peel them.

For the batter, mix the flour, water and salt together in a small bowl, then strain through a fine sieve. Leave to rest for about 20 minutes.

For the sauce, heat a wok or large frying-pan until hot and add the 1 tablespoon of oil. Put in the spring onions, ginger and chilli bean sauce and stir-fry for 30 seconds. Then add the stock, rice wine, vinegar, tomato purée, sugar and soy sauce and continue to cook for 1 minute. Thicken the sauce with the blended cornflour and cook for another minute. Set aside.

Heat the oil in a deep-fat fryer or large wok until quite hot. Dip the slices of aubergine into the batter, let the excess batter drip off, then deep-fry. You may have to do this in several batches. Remove from the oil with a slotted spoon and drain well on kitchen paper.

Arrange the aubergine slices on a serving platter, pour the sauce over and serve.

· S T I R - F R I E D   L E T T U C E ·
Serves 2–4

Lettuce is used so often in the West as a garnish and salad that one tends to forget it is a vegetable and, as such, capable of a greater culinary role. As a child at home, I ate only cooked lettuce and I was a bit put off to see my Western friends eating it raw in their lunch sandwiches. In Hong Kong, the street-side food vendors or food stalls offer stir-fried lettuce as a vegetable dish to accompany rice and chicken dishes. It works very well, provided you use firm lettuce and stir-fry it very quickly.

450 g (1 lb) iceberg or cos lettuce
1 tablespoon oil, preferably groundnut
2 garlic cloves, crushed
1 teaspoon finely chopped fresh ginger

- *3 tablespoons vegetable stock*
- *1 tablespoon light soy sauce*
- *¼ teaspoon salt*
- *1 teaspoon sugar*
- *½ teaspoon cornflour mixed with 1 teaspoon water*

Separate the lettuce leaves and wash well. Cut the large leaves in half.

Heat a wok or large frying-pan and add the oil. When moderately hot, add the garlic and ginger and stir-fry for 30 seconds. Next add the lettuce and stir-fry quickly for a few seconds. Stir in the rest of the ingredients, except the cornflour mixture. Give a couple of stirs and then remove the lettuce to a platter with a slotted spoon. Add the blended cornflour to the sauce and bring to the boil. When the sauce thickens, pour over the lettuce and serve at once.

BITTER MELON WITH BLACK BEAN SAUCE

Serves 2–4

Bitter melon, a type of squash, is one of my favourite Chinese vegetables. True, it has a bitter quinine taste which even many Chinese do not like, but then many Westerners do not like caviar. In China, it is used in its unripe stage, when it is light green and bumpy. There are many ways to prepare it – my mother had a dozen recipes – but the most usual is to cut it up and stir-fry, as in this classic southern Chinese recipe. Look for the riper, softer orange-coloured melons, which tend to be less bitter; the blanching process also reduces the bitterness. In cooking, as often happens, the bitterness is transformed into 'bite' for, while the melon brings out the best flavours of the other ingredients, they in turn seem to neutralize some of its tartness. The result is a surprisingly refreshing effect on the palate. Bitter melon is a taste worth acquiring.

450 g (1 lb) bitter melon
1 tablespoon oil, preferably groundnut
1½ tablespoons black beans, coarsely chopped
1 tablespoon finely chopped fresh ginger
2 teaspoons finely chopped garlic

- 1 tablespoon finely chopped spring onions
- 2 teaspoons light soy sauce
- 1 tablespoon rice wine or dry sherry
- 1 teaspoon sugar
- 150 ml (5 fl oz) vegetable stock

Slice the bitter melon in half lengthways and, using a teaspoon, remove the seeds. Slice the flesh widthwise into about 5 mm (¼ in) pieces. Blanch the bitter melon pieces in a large pan of boiling water for 2 minutes. Drain, plunge them into cold water, then drain in a colander.

Heat a wok or large frying-pan and add the oil. When moderately hot, add the black beans, ginger, garlic and spring onions and stir-fry for 30 seconds. Stir in the soy sauce, rice wine, sugar and stock. Bring the mixture to the boil and add the bitter melon. Continue to cook over high heat for about 3 minutes or until the bitter melon is completely cooked and soft. Serve at once.

CLOUD EARS STIR-FRIED WITH MANGETOUT

Serves 4

This is a colourful and wholesome vegetable dish that is easily assembled for a family dinner. It is a classic combination of the tastes and textures so typical of Chinese cookery. The cloud ears have little flavour of their own but, like mushrooms in general, they readily absorb other flavours and retain their chewy texture. And, like truffles in French cuisine, cloud ears enhance an entire recipe, bringing out the best in the other foods.

15 g (½ oz) Chinese dried cloud ears (black fungus)
100 g (4 oz) fresh or tinned (drained weight) waterchestnuts
100 g (4 oz) celery
1 tablespoon oil, preferably groundnut
2 garlic cloves, crushed
225 g (8 oz) mangetout, trimmed

Sauce
1 teaspoon light soy sauce
1½ tablespoons dark soy sauce
1 teaspoon sugar
2 teaspoons rice wine or dry sherry
2 teaspoons sesame oil
150 ml (5 fl oz) vegetable stock
2 teaspoons cornflour mixed with 2 teaspoons water

Soak the cloud ears in warm water for 20 minutes until soft. Set them aside.

If you are using fresh waterchestnuts, peel them. If you are using tinned waterchestnuts, drain them well and rinse in cold water. Thinly slice the waterchestnuts. String the celery and slice diagonally.

Heat a wok or large frying-pan over a medium heat and add the oil. When hot, add the garlic and stir-fry for 30 seconds. Then add the cloud ears and celery and stir-fry for 2 minutes. Stir in the mangetout and fresh waterchestnuts and stir-fry for another minute. Add all the sauce ingredients, except the blended cornflour. Bring the sauce to the boil and stir in the cornflour mixture. If you are using tinned waterchestnuts, add at this stage and warm through. Turn the mixture onto a serving platter and serve at once.

· CLOUD EARS IN HOISIN SAUCE ·
Serves 4

In this recipe, cloud ears are stir-fried in the strongly flavoured hoisin sauce, which is absorbed thoroughly while the cloud ears still retain their chewy texture. If you wish, you may add another vegetable such as cauliflower or broccoli; but by themselves the cloud ears, given zest by the rich sauce, work very well as a vegetable dish for any meal.

25 g (1 oz) Chinese dried cloud ears (black fungus)
1 tablespoon oil, preferably groundnut
2 garlic cloves, crushed
¼ teaspoon salt
3 tablespoons rice wine or dry sherry

300 ml (10 fl oz) vegetable stock
1 tablespoon light soy sauce
3 tablespoons hoisin sauce
2 teaspoons sesame oil
1 teaspoon cornflour mixed with 1 teaspoon water

Soak the dried cloud ears in warm water for 20 minutes until soft. Rinse in cold water and drain in a colander.

Heat a wok or frying-pan until hot and add the oil and garlic. Stir-fry for 30 seconds, then add the cloud ears. Continue to stir-fry for another 2 minutes. Stir in the rest of the ingredients, except for the cornflour mixture. Continue to cook for another 2 minutes, add the blended cornflour and, when the sauce thickens, the dish is ready to be served.

GRILLED MUSHROOMS WITH LEMON SAUCE

Serves 4

This recipe is of Japanese origin, simple but unusual and quite delicious. It offers a different way to enjoy fresh mushrooms and is a perfect side dish to enliven a barbecue. The mushrooms may also be cooked under the grill, so the dish may be savoured indoors during the winter as well, missing only the smokey barbecue flavour. For an authentic taste, try to obtain Japanese sake for the sauce; if it cannot be found, rice wine or dry sherry are acceptable substitutes. The lemon sauce can be made beforehand.

450 g (1 lb) large button mushrooms
2 teaspoons salt

Sauce
2 tablespoons lemon juice
1 tablespoon dark soy sauce
1 tablespoon sake, rice wine or dry sherry
2 teaspoons sugar
2 tablespoons finely chopped spring onions

Sprinkle the mushrooms with the salt and mix well. Put the mushrooms into a colander and leave to drain for 20 minutes. When the mushrooms have drained, rinse them in water and blot dry with kitchen paper.

Heat the sauce ingredients together in a small pan until the sugar dissolves. Leave to cool.

Soak some wooden skewers in cold water for 5 minutes. Thread 3 or 4 mushrooms on each skewer and cook under the grill or on a barbecue. When they are cooked, remove from the skewers, mix with the sauce and serve.

· STIR-FRIED CUCUMBERS ·
Serves 4

Cucumbers are too often taken for granted, their cool unobtrusive virtues having rendered them less interesting than other vegetables and fit only for salad. Stir-fried, however, they take on an unexpected boldness. My uncle used to cook them with little pieces of pork, but I have learned that they are tasty all by themselves with a complementary sauce. Salt the cucumbers first to rid them of their excess liquid. Stir-fried and made savoury by the sauce, the cucumbers make a wonderful vegetable side dish that is ideal for lunch or dinner.

750 g (1½ lb) cucumbers (about 2 small)	*2 tablespoons dark soy sauce*
2¼ teaspoons salt	*1 tablespoon rice wine or dry sherry*
1 tablespoon oil, preferably groundnut	*2 teaspoons sesame oil*
	1 teaspoon chilli oil

Peel the cucumbers, slice them in half lengthways and, using a teaspoon, remove the seeds. Cut the cucumber halves into 7.5 cm (3 in) lengths. Sprinkle them with 2 teaspoons of the salt and mix well. Put the salted cucumbers into a colander and leave for 20 minutes to drain. This rids the cucumbers of any excess liquid. When the cucumber pieces have drained, rinse in water and then blot dry with kitchen paper.

Heat a wok or large frying-pan until hot and add the oil. Put in the cucumber and stir-fry for 2 minutes. Stir in the remaining salt, soy sauce and rice wine and continue to stir-fry for another 2 minutes. Add the sesame and chilli oils and give the mixture several good stirs. Serve at once.

· STIR-FRIED SPICY CARROTS ·

Serves 4

The European carrot is now the standard in China and in Chinese cookery, although the Chinese do cultivate a larger version which is also quite sweet. Because of their distinctive taste and colour, carrots combine well with other seasonings and herbs, in this case the pungent flavours of ginger, black beans, garlic and dried chillies. The carrots are first roll cut (see p.33) and then blanched. The final step of stir-frying sears the spices and allows the carrots to absorb the new flavours. These colourful and tasty carrots go well with a simple serving of plain rice. They can also be served at room temperature, making them an interesting addition to any picnic menu.

750 g (1½ lb) carrots
1 tablespoon oil, preferably groundnut
2 teaspoons finely chopped garlic
1 teaspoon finely chopped fresh ginger
2 dried chillies, seeded

1 tablespoon black beans, coarsely chopped
1 teaspoon sugar
2 tablespoons rice wine or dry sherry
2 teaspoons sesame oil

Peel the carrots and roll cut according to the technique on p.33. Blanch the carrots in a large pan of boiling salted water for 4–5 minutes, then immerse them in cold water. Drain thoroughly.

Heat a wok or large frying-pan until moderately hot and add the oil. Put in the garlic, ginger, chillies and black beans and stir-fry for about 1 minute. Stir in the carrots, sugar and rice wine and continue to stir-fry for about 3 minutes or until the carrots are thoroughly heated. Add the sesame oil and continue to stir-fry for 20 seconds.

CRISPY SPRING ONION OMELETTE

Serves 2

Here the mildness and soft texture of the eggs are transformed by the cooking process and the addition of other textures and seasonings. My mother often prepared just such a dish when she was in a hurry, as it was quick and economical. It would be served over rice, with a touch of soy sauce.

6 spring onions
15 g (½ oz) fresh chilli
6 eggs, beaten
1 tablespoon sesame oil
3 tablespoons finely chopped spring onions
½ teaspoon salt

2 teaspoons light soy sauce
4 tablespoons oil, preferably groundnut

Garnish
1 tablespoon finely chopped fresh coriander

Cut the spring onions diagonally into 5 cm (2 in) lengths. Finely shred the chilli. In a large bowl, mix the eggs, sesame oil, finely chopped spring onions, salt and soy sauce.

Heat a wok or large frying-pan over high heat and add 1 tablespoon of the oil. Put in the spring onion pieces and chilli and stir-fry for 2 minutes. Remove them and wipe the wok clean. Re-heat the wok and add the 3 tablespoons of oil and, when hot, add the egg mixture. When the egg begins to cook, return the cooked spring onions and chilli to the wok and continue to cook over high heat for 2 minutes until brown and crispy. Flip the omelette over and brown the other side. Remove to a platter and garnish with the coriander. Serve at once.

BRAISED CHINESE MUSHROOMS

Serves 4

Chinese family banquets, held on special occasions, are truly feasts. As a boy attending such gala affairs, I always looked for the large plate of beautifully arranged, thick Chinese mushrooms that traditionally graced the table. Braised in a rich sauce, smokey in taste, chewy in texture, these mushrooms were a great favourite of mine. I ate them whenever I could, as any Western youth might eat crisps or roasted peanuts. The large dried variety of Chinese mushrooms recommended for this recipe can be expensive, but they are well worth it for a special occasion. Do not cut up the caps, as left whole they absorb the sauce better. The dish re-heats beautifully, which makes it ideal for a large dinner party as it can be prepared in advance.

100 g (4 oz) large Chinese dried mushrooms	*2 tablespoons sugar*
1 tablespoon oil, preferably groundnut	*2 teaspoons sesame oil*
	1 tablespoon rice wine or dry sherry
Sauce	**Garnish**
300 ml (10 fl oz) vegetable stock	*2 spring onions, sliced*
2 tablespoons dark soy sauce	

Soak the dried mushrooms in warm water for 20 minutes until soft. Squeeze the excess liquid from the mushrooms and remove and discard the stalks. Leave the mushrooms whole.

Heat a wok or large frying-pan and add the oil. Put in the mushrooms and stir-fry for a few seconds. Quickly add the sauce ingredients and turn the heat down. Braise the mushrooms for 7 minutes, stirring continually, until the mushrooms have absorbed most of the sauce. Turn the mixture onto a serving platter and garnish with the spring onions.

EGGS WITH CHINESE MUSHROOMS

Serves 4

Eggs are popular in Eastern cookery. In China, the tradition is to contrast the softness of the eggs with firm or crisp textures. In this recipe, I combine two varieties of dried firm mushrooms, one of them cloud ears, with eggs. Do try to obtain the Chinese variety. You may use fresh button mushrooms, but be sure to cook them until most of the moisture has gone. This is easy to prepare and goes wonderfully with rice or as a filling for Chinese Pancakes (see p.41).

25 g (1 oz) Chinese dried mushrooms
15 g (½ oz) Chinese dried cloud ears (black fungus)
225 g (8 oz) onions
4 eggs, beaten
2½ teaspoons salt
1 tablespoon sesame oil
3 tablespoons oil, preferably groundnut

2 tablespoons rice wine or dry sherry
1 tablespoon light soy sauce
3 tablespoons vegetable stock

Garnish
3 tablespoons chopped spring onions
1 teaspoon sesame oil

Soak the Chinese dried mushrooms and cloud ears in separate bowls of warm water for about 20 minutes, then drain. Rinse the cloud ears well and leave whole. Squeeze out any excess liquid from the dried mushrooms, discard the tough stalks, then shred the caps and set aside. Finely slice the onions. Combine the eggs with 2 teaspoons of the salt and sesame oil in a small bowl.

Heat a wok or large frying-pan over high heat and add 1 tablespoon of the oil. Put in the onions and stir-fry for 4 minutes until soft and translucent. Remove them and wipe the wok clean. Re-heat the wok over high heat and add the remaining oil. Add the mushrooms, cloud ears, rice wine, soy sauce and remaining salt and stir-fry for 2 minutes. Stir in the stock and return the cooked onions to the wok. Continue to stir-fry for 1 minute. Then add the egg mixture and stir several times. The dish is ready when the eggs have set. Transfer to a platter and garnish with the spring onions and sesame oil.

· CRISPY VEGETABLE STIR-FRY
Serves 4

I like to serve meals that appeal to the eye as well as to the pala
Therefore, when peppers are in season I use them as often as possibl
the sweetness of the reds and yellows and the mild bite of the greer
delight one's senses and add a colourful dimension to any meal. Stir
frying preserves the best characteristics of peppers. When combined
as here, with the crisp texture and sweet flavour of bamboo shoots
and waterchestnuts and the zing of ginger, the result is a colourful and
healthy vegetable dish. Use fresh waterchestnuts if possible.

Remember that the key to stir-frying vegetables is to cook the
harder ones, or those with the least amount of moisture, first.

100 g (4 oz) red peppers	*2 teaspoons oil, preferably*
100 g (4 oz) green peppers	*groundnut*
100 g (4 oz) yellow peppers	*2 teaspoons salt*
100 g (4 oz) fresh or tinned	*3 slices fresh ginger*
(drained weight) waterchestnuts	*50 g (2 oz) mangetout, trimmed*
50 g (2 oz) tinned (drained weight)	*3 tablespoons water*
bamboo shoots	

Cut the peppers into 3.5 cm (1½ in) triangles. Thinly slice the
waterchestnuts and bamboo shoots.

Heat a wok or large frying-pan and add the oil. When moderately
hot, add the salt and ginger and stir-fry for about 1 minute to allow
the ginger to flavour the oil. Add the peppers and stir-fry for 2 minutes.
Stir in the waterchestnuts and bamboo shoots and continue to stir-fry
for 2 minutes. Finally add the mangetout and stir-fry for 30 seconds,
then add the water. Stir-fry for another minute or until the mangetout
are cooked, adding more water if necessary. When the vegetables are
cooked, serve them at once.

VIETNAMESE-STYLE VEGETABLES

Serves 4

This is a home-style family dish that is also served in Vietnamese restaurants. Its main ingredients are nutritious beancurd and mushrooms, combined with cauliflower, which provides a new texture and flavour, and a spicy light soy sauce to enliven the dish. The beancurd, cut into thin strips and deep-fried, does not break up when stir-fried. Serve this substantial dish with plain rice and you have a complete meal.

225 g (8 oz) fresh beancurd
300 ml (10 fl oz) oil, preferably groundnut, for deep-frying
100 g (4 oz) cauliflower
1½ tablespoons oil, preferably groundnut
2 garlic cloves, crushed
2 tablespoons finely chopped shallots

225 g (8 oz) small button mushrooms
½ teaspoon salt
150 ml (5 fl oz) water
2 tablespoons light soy sauce
3 tablespoons finely chopped fresh coriander

Cut the beancurd into 7.5 × 1 cm (3 × ½ in) strips.

Heat the 300 ml (10 fl oz) of oil in a deep-fat fryer or a large wok until it almost smokes. Deep-fry the beancurd strips in two batches. When each batch is light brown, remove and drain the beancurd well on kitchen paper.

Cut the cauliflower into small florets about 2.5–3.5 cm (1–1½ in) wide. Blanch the florets in a large pan of boiling salted water for several minutes, then immerse in cold water and drain thoroughly.

Heat a wok or large frying-pan and add the 1½ tablespoons of oil. Put in the garlic and shallots and stir-fry for 30 seconds. Then add the mushrooms, salt, water and soy sauce and stir-fry for 5 minutes. Gently stir in the beancurd, cauliflower and fresh coriander and continue to stir-fry for 2 minutes or until the cauliflower and beancurd are heated through. It is then ready to serve.

pepper and stir well. Stir the blended cornflour into the sauce and bring it back to the boil. Reduce the heat to simmering point and gently put in the beancurd and pineapple. Mix well, then turn the mixture onto a deep platter. Garnish and serve at once.

SIMPLE BEANCURD AND MUSHROOM STIR-FRY

Serves 2–4

In this healthy family dish, the lightly fried beancurd with a slightly crispy surface sets off the texture of the braised mushrooms perfectly. Remember to fry the delicate beancurd squares gently. This dish re-heats well and is even better the second day, although of course some of the crispness will be lost.

450 g (1 lb) firm beancurd
4 tablespoons oil, preferably groundnut
2 garlic cloves, crushed
¼ teaspoon salt
225 g (8 oz) small whole button mushrooms

Sauce
1 tablespoon dark soy sauce
2 tablespoons rice wine or dry sherry
2 tablespoons sugar
2 tablespoons vegetable stock

Garnish
2 spring onions, diagonally sliced

Cut the beancurd into 5 cm (2 in) squares, 1 cm (½ in) thick.

Heat a wok or large frying-pan and add 3 tablespoons of the oil. When the oil is hot, fry the beancurd on each side until golden brown. You may have to do this in several batches. Drain on kitchen paper.

Drain the oil and wipe the wok clean. Re-heat the wok over moderate heat and add the remaining tablespoon of oil. Put in the garlic and salt and stir-fry for 30 seconds. Stir in the mushrooms and the sauce ingredients. Cook over moderate heat for 5 minutes or until the mushrooms are cooked. Return the beancurd to the wok and, once heated through, garnish and serve.

· STUFFED BEANCURD SQUARES ·

Serves 2–4

Beancurd suffers from an undeserved reputation for excessive bland-ness and dullness. It is indeed bland (and so is rice), but this is a virtue when properly approached. The trick is to take advantage of beancurd's generous receptivity to other foods, spices and seasonings. In this recipe, which my cooking colleague Gordon Wing helped to create, we stuffed the beancurd with a mixture of ginger, mushrooms, onions, and other flavours and textures, then pan-fried and covered the beancurd squares with a savoury sauce. Serve with rice.

450 g (1 lb) firm beancurd
3–4 tablespoons oil, preferably groundnut

Filling
15 g (½ oz) Chinese dried mushrooms
1 teaspoon finely chopped spring onions
½ teaspoon finely chopped fresh ginger
3 tablespoons roasted peanuts, coarsely chopped
½ teaspoon salt
½ teaspoon pepper

1 teaspoon sugar
1 teaspoon yellow bean sauce
2 tablespoons coarsely chopped garlic
½ teaspoon Sichuan peppercorns, roasted and ground (see p.24)

Sauce
1 tablespoon dark soy sauce
1 tablespoon light soy sauce
1 tablespoon rice wine or dry sherry
½ teaspoon cornflour mixed with 3 tablespoons water

Soak the dried mushrooms in a bowl of warm water for 20 minutes. Drain and squeeze out any excess liquid. Cut off and discard the stalks; coarsely chop the mushroom caps.

Cut the beancurd into 4 pieces to make squares. With a teaspoon, scoop out 1 tablespoon of beancurd from the top, without breaking through to the bottom. You will now have a square of beancurd with a dip in the centre of the top. This is where the filling will go.

Heat a wok or large frying-pan over moderate heat and add 1 tablespoon of the oil. Put in the filling ingredients and stir-fry for 2 minutes. Leave the mixture to cool, then finely chop in a blender. Gently spoon the filling into the hollowed-out beancurd squares.

Heat a frying-pan or wok over high heat and add 2 tablespoons of the oil. When hot, add the stuffed beancurd squares, unfilled side down. Lower the heat and fry, turning them over from time to time until they are brown all over. You may have to do this in batches, adding more oil if necessary. Remove the stuffed beancurd, drain on kitchen paper, and arrange on a serving platter.

Meanwhile, wipe out the wok and bring the sauce ingredients to simmering point, stirring. Pour this mixture over the beancurd and serve at once.

SAVOURY BEANCURD CASSEROLE

Serves 4

There are many different variations of beancurd, and one of the tastiest is fermented red beancurd. This impressive condiment is preserved by fermentation in a solution of red rice, salt and spices. It has a pungent aroma which dissipates as it cooks, leaving a flavour and fragrance that richly complements a stew or casserole, especially one made with beancurd. The strong flavours also permeate the noodles. My mother often made a version of this casserole during the cold Chicago winters of my childhood. Its rich aromas and combination of flavours evoke memories of those days. This is a hearty dish that re-heats easily and is perfect served over rice.

- 25 g (1 oz) Chinese dried mushrooms
- 350 g (12 oz) Chinese leaves or white cabbage
- 450 g (1 lb) firm beancurd
- 450 ml (15 fl oz) oil, preferably groundnut, for deep-frying
- 1 tablespoon oil, preferably groundnut
- 2 tablespoons fermented red beancurd
- 1 tablespoon finely chopped fresh ginger
- 1½ tablespoons finely chopped garlic
- 50 g (2 oz) bean thread (transparent) noodles
- 1 teaspoon salt
- 2 teaspoons sugar
- 3 tablespoons rice wine or dry sherry
- 1 tablespoon light soy sauce
- 3 tablespoons chopped spring onions
- 300 ml (10 fl oz) vegetable stock

Soak the dried mushrooms in warm water for about 20 minutes until soft. Squeeze the excess liquid from the mushrooms, and remove and discard the stalks. Shred the Chinese leaves or white cabbage.

Cut the beancurd into 2.5 cm (1 in) cubes. Heat the oil in a deep-fat fryer or large wok. When the oil is almost smoking, deep-fry the beancurd cubes. You may have to do this in several batches. Remove and drain on kitchen paper.

Heat a wok or large frying-pan and add the 1 tablespoon of oil. Put in the fermented beancurd, ginger and garlic and stir-fry for about 30 seconds. Add the rest of the ingredients. Bring the mixture to simmering point and add the deep-fried beancurd. Cover tightly and braise gently for about 20 minutes.

To re-heat, bring to simmering point over low heat until the mixture is hot.

CANTONESE-STYLE BEANCURD WITH CHINESE GREENS

Serves 2–4

This tasty dish is a staple item on the food stalls and in the kitchens of Hong Kong. It is nutritious, inexpensive and substantial. Chinese greens have a light, earthy, fresh taste and go well with beancurd. This is an easy-to-make treat, and when served with plain rice makes a full meal. You may substitute Swiss chard or spinach for the Chinese greens.

450 g (1 lb) firm beancurd
450 g (1 lb) Chinese greens
300 ml (10 fl oz) oil, preferably groundnut, for deep-frying
1 tablespoon oil, preferably groundnut

- *4 garlic cloves, crushed*
- *3 tablespoons dark soy sauce*
- *150 ml (5 fl oz) vegetable stock*
- *1 tablespoon cornflour mixed with*
- *1 tablespoon water*

Cut the beancurd into 2.5 cm (1 in) cubes. Cut the Chinese greens into 7.5 cm (3 in) strips.

Heat the 300 ml (10 fl oz) of oil in a deep-fat fryer or large wok until it almost smokes. Deep-fry the beancurd cubes in several batches. When each batch of beancurd cubes is lightly browned, about 1–2 minutes, remove and drain well on kitchen paper.

Heat a wok or large frying-pan and add the 1 tablespoon of oil. When hot, put in the garlic and Chinese greens and stir-fry for 2 minutes over high heat. Stir in the soy sauce, stock and blended cornflour. Reduce the heat to very low and add the beancurd cubes. Simmer for 3 minutes or until the beancurd is heated through.

COCONUT-STEWED BEANCURD AND VEGETABLES

Serves 4

Vegetable stews enjoy an honourable place in the Chinese cuisine and are popular throughout Southeast Asia. Meat and poultry are often expensive, but the cheaper beancurd and vegetables provide a healthy and flavoursome substitute. They are the principal dishes today for most rural Indonesian families and, in Thailand, they are prominent among the non-curry meals available at food stalls. This unusual recipe is of Vietnamese origin. The beancurd is deep-fried and then braised with vegetables in a rich coconut milk broth flavoured with soy sauce. You may substitute other vegetables, such as Brussels sprouts, turnips or parsnips if you like – always use those that are in season. As with stews in general, vegetable stews can be made well in advance, and they taste better the day after preparation – but re-heat them slowly. Serve with plain rice.

450 g (1 lb) firm beancurd	450 ml (15 fl oz) fresh or tinned
225 g (8 oz) cauliflower	coconut milk (see p.14)
100 g (4 oz) Chinese long beans,	150 ml (5 fl oz) water
runner beans or French beans,	½ teaspoon salt
trimmed	2 tablespoons dark soy sauce
100 g (4 oz) carrots	1 tablespoon light soy sauce
100 g (4 oz) fresh or frozen peas	2 teaspoons sugar
300 ml (10 fl oz) oil, preferably	
groundnut, for deep-frying	

Cut the beancurd into 2.5 cm (1 in) cubes. Cut the cauliflower into small florets about 2.5–3.5 cm (1–1½ in) wide. Slice the beans into 7.5 cm (3 in) lengths. Peel and cut the carrots into 1 cm (½ in) cubes. If you are using fresh peas, blanch them for 3 minutes in a pan of boiling water, then drain in a colander. (There is no need to blanch the frozen peas.)

Heat the oil in a deep-fat fryer or a large wok until it almost smokes. Deep-fry the beancurd cubes for 1–2 minutes in two batches. When each batch of beancurd cubes is lightly brown, remove and drain well on kitchen paper.

Bring the coconut milk, water, salt, soy sauces and sugar to the boil in a large pan. Reduce the heat to simmering, add the vegetables and beancurd, cover tightly and braise for about 20 minutes or until the vegetables are cooked.

· R E D - C O O K E D   B E A N C U R D ·
Serves 2–4

'Red-cooked' is a term applied to Chinese dishes braised and spiced with the robust, dark, brownish-red seasonings of hoisin sauce, made from soya bean flour, red beans, chillies, sugar, salt, garlic and spices. The fried beancurd has a crispy surface while its soft interior readily absorbs the sauce. This is a flavourful dish that is a complete meal with other vegetables and plain rice.

450 g (1 lb) firm beancurd
3 tablespoons oil, preferably groundnut

Sauce
2 tablespoons dark soy sauce
1 tablespoon rice wine or dry sherry
½ teaspoon Sichuan peppercorns, roasted and finely ground (see p.24)

- *2 tablespoons hoisin sauce*
- *1 teaspoon chilli bean sauce*
- *1 teaspoon sugar*
- *2 teaspoons finely chopped fresh ginger*
- *¼ teaspoon salt*
- *150 ml (5 fl oz) vegetable stock*
- *1 tablespoon oil, preferably groundnut*

Cut the beancurd into 2.5 cm (1 in) cubes. Heat a wok or large frying-pan and add the oil. When moderately hot, add the beancurd and fry for 1–2 minutes on each side until golden brown. Set aside. Wipe the wok clean.

Add all the sauce ingredients to the wok and bring to simmering point. Return the beancurd to the wok and simmer gently in this mixture for about 5 minutes. Turn onto a serving platter and serve.

CRISPY BEANCURD CUBES WITH PEANUT DIPPING SAUCE

Serves 4–6

In this delectable recipe, based on a dish I once enjoyed in Thailand, the peanut dipping sauce provides the zest and colour for the beancurd. In Thailand, roasted peanuts are pounded into a paste which is much easier to use than our peanut butter; some little bits of peanut are left in the paste to provide a crunchy texture. Here, the fried cubes of beancurd, crusty on the outside and spongy soft inside, are dipped into the peanut sauce, making a delightful starter or cocktail food. Serve the beancurd hot, as its skin toughens as it cools.

350 g (12 oz) firm beancurd
300 ml (10 fl oz) oil, preferably groundnut, for deep-frying

Sauce
25 g (1 oz) roasted peanuts
1 tablespoon sugar

2 tablespoons water
2 teaspoons Chinese white rice vinegar or cider vinegar
1 tablespoon finely chopped fresh coriander
½ teaspoon salt
½ teaspoon chilli oil

Cut the beancurd into 2.5 cm (1 in) cubes. Combine the sauce ingredients together in a small bowl and set aside.

Heat the oil in a deep-fat fryer or large wok until it almost smokes. Deep-fry the beancurd cubes for 1–2 minutes in two batches. When each batch of beancurd cubes is lightly browned, remove and drain well on kitchen paper.

Arrange the beancurd cubes on a platter and serve the peanut sauce separately for dipping.

OPPOSITE: **Singapore Noodles** *(page 171)*

DINNER IN A HURRY FOR TWO OR MORE
Spinach and Egg-Ribbon Soup *(page 75)*
Sesame Buckwheat Noodles *(page 180)*
Stir-Fried Lettuce *(page 121)*

PAN-FRIED BEANCURD WITH LEEKS

Serves 2–4

Leeks are popular throughout China but especially in the north, where this recipe comes from. They are an ideal accompaniment to beancurd because of their texture and robust flavour. This is good, simple fare of the kind Chinese families enjoy at home. Serve with plain boiled rice.

450 g (1 lb) firm beancurd
3 tablespoons oil, preferably groundnut
350 g (12 oz) leeks
3 garlic cloves, crushed
1 dried chilli, seeded

- *2 teaspoons chilli bean sauce*
- *1½ tablespoons dark soy sauce*
- *2 teaspoons sugar*
- *1 tablespoon rice wine or dry sherry*
- *150 ml (5 fl oz) vegetable stock*

Cut the beancurd in half, then cut again on the diagonal into triangles. Heat a wok or large frying-pan over moderate heat and add the oil. Fry the beancurd triangles until golden brown. You may have to do this in several batches. Drain on kitchen paper.

Cut the leeks into shreds, discarding the green parts. Wash well; you may have to do this several times.

Re-heat the wok over high heat. Put in the garlic and chilli and stir-fry for 30 seconds. Add the leeks and continue to stir-fry for 3 minutes, then add the rest of the ingredients. Bring the mixture to the boil. Turn the heat down to a simmer and return the beancurd triangles to the mixture. Cook for another 3 minutes or until the beancurd is heated through. Serve at once.

OPPOSITE: Chinese Toffee Apples *(page 203)* and Rice Puffs with Prune Filling *(page 207)*

BEANCURD CUSTARD IN SOY SAUCE

Serves 2–4

For a high-protein vegetarian main dish, try this simple recipe. Served with fresh vegetables and plain rice, you have a wholesome family meal. The soft beancurd must be handled more gently than the firm variety, but it will be like eating a wonderful silky, savoury custard. Always use the freshest beancurd available.

450 g (1 lb) soft beancurd
1 tablespoon oil, preferably groundnut
2 slices fresh ginger
2½ tablespoons dark soy sauce
1 teaspoon light soy sauce

- *1 tablespoon rice wine or dry sherry*
- *150 ml (5 fl oz) vegetable stock*
- *1 teaspoon sugar*
- *1 teaspoon cornflour mixed with 1 teaspoon water*

Cut the beancurd into 3.5 cm (1½ in) cubes.

Heat a wok or large frying-pan and add the oil. When moderately hot, add the ginger slices, soy sauces, rice wine, stock and sugar and stir for 1 minute, then add the blended cornflour. When the mixture begins to thicken, add the beancurd and simmer gently to heat through. Serve at once.

CHAPTER SIX

HOT PASTA AND NOODLES

Pasta or noodles come in many forms in China, Japan and Southeast Asia. I need only name the various types of Japanese pasta to illustrate: harusame, hiyamugi, kishimen, malfun, ramen, shiratake, soba, somen, udon. *These are made from wheat, rice, buckwheat, bean threads or yam threads. Throughout these areas, pasta is eaten in the form of noodles, wontons and pasta wrappers. These foods have been a part of the diet of this region for many hundreds of years.*

All pasta is characterized by subtle variations of texture and colour, absorbent receptivity to sauces and congeniality to other foods, plus excellent nutritional values. Its universal popularity is therefore not surprising.

The word 'pasta' is, of course, an Italian word. I use it because it has entered our language as a generic term meaning unleavened dough, rolled out and formed into different shapes. One regional difference is that some oriental pastas are made from rice flour rather than wheat.

In this book, I have combined various pastas with spices and flavours typical of China, Japan and Southeast Asia. I have included as well some East–West blends. The dishes are wholesome, sustaining, light and relatively easy to make. They may serve as starters, side dishes or complete meals in themselves. Make and savour them, and they will immediately become a regular part of your diet.

Although there are many types of pasta noodles found in China, Japan and Southeast Asia, not all of them are easily available in the West. Therefore, I have restricted myself to those which are dried and can be found in Chinese, oriental or Asian grocers. Some cannot be found in supermarkets but are easily obtained in these more specialist shops.

Here are some of the most common types of noodle available:

Wheat Noodles and Egg Noodles

These are made from hard or soft wheat flour and water. If egg has been added, the noodles are usually labelled as egg noodles. They can be bought dried or fresh from Chinese and oriental grocers, and many supermarkets and delicatessens also stock the dried variety. Flat noodles are usually used in soups, and rounded noodles are best for stir-frying. If you can't get Chinese noodles, you can use Italian egg noodles (dried or fresh) instead.

To cook wheat and egg noodles

Noodles are very good boiled and served instead of plain rice with main dishes. I think dried wheat or fresh egg noodles are best for this. If you are using fresh noodles, immerse them in a pan of boiling water and cook for 3–5 minutes or until they are soft. If you are using dried noodles, either cook them according to the instructions on the packet, or cook in boiling water for 4–5 minutes. Drain and serve.

If you are cooking noodles ahead of time before using them in another dish or before stir-frying them, toss the cooked drained noodles in a teaspoon or two of sesame oil and put them into a bowl. Cover this with cling film and put it in the fridge. The cooked noodles will remain usable for about 2 hours.

Udon noodles

Udon are Japanese wheat noodles and can sometimes be found fresh at some supermarkets or Chinese or oriental grocers. Round or flat, they can be purchased dried and should be cooked until they are soft but not overcooked, so they still retain a little bite.

Buckwheat noodles

These Japanese noodles are thin and a brownish grey colour. Known as *soba* and extremely popular among the Japanese, they are often eaten as snacks, served cold in the summer and hot in the winter. They come fresh and dried, and can be found where Japanese food products are sold.

RICE NOODLES

Rice noodles are popular in southern China and throughout Southeast Asia. They are usually dried and can be found in Chinese and oriental grocers. Rice noodles are white and come in a variety of shapes. One of the most common is rice stick noodles, which are flat and about the length of a chopstick. They can also vary in thickness. Use the type called for in the recipe. Rice noodles are very easy to use. Simply soak them in warm water for 15 minutes or until they are soft. Drain them in a colander or sieve and they are then ready to be used in soups or to be stir-fried. Fresh rice noodles, which can also be found in Chinese and oriental grocers, are a popular type called 'fun noodles'. These need to be cooked straight away.

'Fun' rice noodles

The Chinese make large sheets of rice noodles from a basic mixture of rice flour, wheat *starch* (not flour) and water. This pasta is then steamed in sheets. When cooked, the sheets are cut into noodles to be eaten immediately. A very popular street snack in China, Hong Kong and Singapore, the fresh noodles are most often served with a sauce.

RICE PAPERS

Vietnamese rice papers are often beautifully textured by the imprint of the bamboo trays on which they are placed to dry. They are very thin dried sheets, usually round, and are used as wrappers for a Vietnamese-style spring roll. The dried sheets are very briefly soaked in water to soften them, then rolled around a filling and deep-fried to a light and crispy texture. Unlike the Chinese wrappers, the filled rice papers can be stored in the fridge for up to 3 hours before frying. Once they are fried, they can be kept crisp in a low oven for up to 2 hours.

Bean Thread (Transparent) Noodles

These noodles, also called cellophane noodles, are made from ground mung beans and not from a grain flour. They are available dried, and are very fine and white. Easy to recognize packed in their neat, plastic-wrapped bundles, they are stocked by most Chinese grocers and some supermarkets. They are never served on their own, but are added to soups or braised dishes or are deep-fried as a garnish. They must be soaked in warm water for about 5 minutes before use. As they are rather long, you might find it easier to cut them into shorter lengths after soaking. They can also be fried, in which case do not soak them before using.

FRESH PASTA WITH CORIANDER, GINGER AND BASIL PESTO

Serves 6

This recipe was inspired by a colleague, Bruce Cost. A superb chef and author of excellent cookery books, one of his specialities is the food of Southeast Asia. Here, I elaborate on a version of his delicious Asian pesto. Pesto is an Italian term meaning any sauce whose ingredients have been pounded and mixed together. The original Genoan pesto sauce consists of fresh basil, Parmesan cheese, oil and garlic pounded into a smooth green paste. Ordinary fresh basil may be used here but, if you can, try to obtain the Asian tropical variety which has a distinctive basil-anise flavour worth savouring. Fresh coriander and ginger are, of course, traditional oriental seasonings. Combine this pesto with your own freshly made pasta, or buy dried or freshly made Chinese egg noodles.

275 g (10 oz) plain flour
3 size 1 eggs
2 tablespoons oil, preferably groundnut
1 teaspoon salt

Sauce
1 tablespoon finely chopped fresh ginger
1 tablespoon finely chopped fresh coriander

- *3 tablespoons finely chopped fresh basil*
- *2 tablespoons finely chopped garlic*
- *1 tablespoon oil, preferably groundnut*
- *2 teaspoons sesame oil*
- *2 teaspoons salt*
- *1 teaspoon freshly ground black pepper*

For the pasta, by hand or in a food processor, combine the flour, eggs, oil and salt. Knead the dough until smooth and satiny. Run the pasta through a pasta machine twice on each setting, stopping at the thinnest setting. Cut the pasta into thin noodles. Flour lightly and set aside.

Combine all the sauce ingredients and mix thoroughly in a blender. Set aside.

Bring a large pan of water to the boil. Add the pasta and cook for 1 minute. Drain thoroughly and toss with the sauce. Serve at once.

SPICY BEAN THREAD NOODLES WITH PRESERVED VEGETABLES

Serves 2–4

These noodles have a smooth, light texture that readily absorbs the surrounding flavours. Because most of the work involved can be done the day before and because the dish re-heats so well, this may be called gourmet fast food. But take care when cooking the noodles because if they overcook they tend to lump together. Although the bean thread are known as noodles, the dish is delicious served with rice also.

25 g (1 oz) Chinese dried mushrooms

175 g (6 oz) bean thread (transparent) noodles

2 tablespoons oil, preferably groundnut

2 tablespoons finely chopped garlic

1 tablespoon finely chopped fresh ginger

2 tablespoons finely chopped shallots

2 teaspoons chilli bean sauce

50 g (2 oz) Sichuan preserved vegetables, rinsed and finely chopped

2 teaspoons light soy sauce

2 teaspoons sugar

2 tablespoons rice wine or dry sherry

2 teaspoons chilli oil

Garnish

3 tablespoons finely chopped spring onions, green part only

Soak the dried mushrooms in warm water for 20 minutes. Drain them, squeeze out any excess liquid, cut off and discard the stalks and coarsely chop the mushrooms caps. Soak the noodles in a large bowl of warm water for 15 minutes. When soft, drain the noodles well. Cut into 7.5 cm (3 in) lengths, using scissors or a knife.

Heat a wok or pan and add the oil. Put in the garlic, ginger, shallot and chilli bean sauce and stir-fry quickly for a few seconds. Add the vegetables, mushrooms and noodles and stir-fry for about 2 minutes. Stir in the soy sauce, sugar, rice wine and chilli oil and continue to cook the mixture over a gentle heat for about 5 minutes. Ladle the noodles into a large serving bowl, garnish with the spring onions and serve at once.

· SPINACH AND RICE NOODLES ·
Serves 2–4

In this quick and healthy light meal, the dried noodles need only to be soaked and require very little cooking. Their texture is such that the spinach flavour, some of the colour and other seasonings are readily absorbed. Unlike egg noodles, rice noodles do not become sticky and gummy when they are moist; this makes it convenient to serve them cold. I add a little sugar to neutralize the iron and salt taste of the spinach.

750 g (1½ lb) fresh spinach
100 g (4 oz) rice noodles, rice vermicelli or rice sticks
1 tablespoon oil, preferably groundnut
1 teaspoon salt

- *2 tablespoons coarsely chopped garlic*
- *2 teaspoons sugar*
- *1 tablespoon light soy sauce*
- *2 teaspoons chilli oil*

Wash the spinach thoroughly. Remove all the stalks, leaving just the leaves.

Soak the rice noodles in a bowl of warm water for 25 minutes. Then drain them in a colander or sieve. If you are using dried egg noodles, cook them for 3–5 minutes in boiling water, drain then immerse in cold water until required.

Heat a wok or large pan to moderate heat and add the oil. Put in the salt and garlic and stir-fry for a few seconds. Add the spinach leaves and stir-fry for 2 minutes to coat the spinach leaves thoroughly. When the spinach has wilted to about a third of its original size, add the rice noodles, sugar, soy sauce and chilli oil, and continue to stir-fry for another 4 minutes. Transfer the noodles to a plate, and pour off any excess liquid. Serve hot or cold.

KOREAN BEAN THREAD SESAME NOODLES WITH VEGETABLES

Serves 4

Bean thread noodles are made from the starch of the mung bean and, when cooked, they are almost transparent. This simple to prepare recipe is my version of a popular Korean dish. What makes it memorable is the combination of lace-like noodles and exotic mushrooms, an unusual mixture of tastes and textures. The dried mushrooms and cloud ears are available at Chinese grocers and it is well worth the effort to obtain them.

25 g (1 oz) Chinese dried
mushrooms
15 g (½ oz) Chinese dried cloud
ears (black fungus)
100 g (4 oz) bean thread
(transparent) noodles
50 g (2 oz) carrot
1 green pepper
1 small onion
2 tablespoons oil, preferably
groundnut
120 ml (4 fl oz) water

Sauce
2 tablespoons light soy sauce
2 tablespoons dark soy sauce
3 tablespoons sesame oil
1½ tablespoons sesame seeds
1 tablespoon finely chopped garlic
1 tablespoon sugar
1 teaspoon freshly ground black
pepper

Soak the dried mushrooms in warm water for 20 minutes until soft. Squeeze the excess liquid from the mushrooms and remove and discard the stalks. Cut the caps into shreds. Soak the cloud ears in warm water for about 20 minutes or until soft. Rinse them well in cold water and drain thoroughly in a colander.

Soak the noodles in a large bowl of very hot water for 15 minutes. When soft, drain well. Cut the noodles into 7.5 cm (3 in) lengths, using scissors or a knife.

Peel and finely shred the carrot. Finely shred the pepper and onion.

Heat a wok or large frying-pan and add the oil. When moderately hot, add the mushrooms, cloud ears, carrot, onion, green pepper and water and stir-fry for 5 minutes or until the carrots are cooked.

Combine the sauce ingredients and add them to the vegetables. Give the mixture a good stir, then add the noodles. Stir-fry the mixture for 2 minutes until well heated through. Serve at once or at room temperature.

· UDON NOODLES IN BROTH ·
Serves 4

During my student days I became a devotee of Japanese films, especially those that incidentally depicted scenes from daily life. Such films gave me insight into a culture that I had only read about and never directly experienced. Naturally, I was particularly interested in scenes showing eating habits and cookery. I noticed that the Japanese often seemed to be snacking on soup noodles, slurping them up and smacking their lips in a way that always made me hungry. I later learned that these were probably *udon* noodles, a Japanese favourite. Made from bleached white flour with no eggs, these noodles are very white and fine and vary in thickness. In an easy soup such as this, they make a hearty lunch.

350 g (12 oz) dried udon noodles (see p.156)
225 g (8 oz) fresh or tinned tomatoes
8 spring onions

- *1.2 litres (2 pints) vegetable stock*
- *2 teaspoons salt*
- *1 teaspoon freshly ground white pepper*

Cook the noodles in a saucepan of boiling water for 4–5 minutes or according to the instructions on the packet. Drain the noodles, then put them into cold water until required.

If you are using fresh tomatoes, skin, seed and cut into 2.5 cm (1 in) cubes. If you are using tinned tomatoes, chop them into small chunks. Cut the spring onions diagonally into 7.5 cm (3 in) lengths.

Put the stock into a saucepan and bring to simmering point. Add the salt and pepper and simmer for 2 minutes. Stir in the noodles and tomatoes and simmer until heated through. Add the spring onions and simmer for a further 30 seconds, then serve.

CRISPY CANTONESE-STYLE NOODLES WITH VEGETABLES

Serves 2–4

The origins of pasta are obscured by time and controversy, but there is a general consensus that the Chinese first thought of the egg noodle variety. Whoever invented the process, pan-fried noodles make a perfect foundation for stir-fried dishes. Here, the pan-frying technique leaves the noodles brown, firm and crispy on the outside and yellow, moist and soft on the inside, a combination of textures that is classically Chinese. Upon this noodle base is placed stir-fried vegetables topped with a zesty sauce.

25 g (1 oz) button mushrooms	100 g (4 oz) mangetout, trimmed
6 spring onions	2 teaspoons light soy sauce
100 g (4 oz) red pepper	2 tablespoons dark soy sauce
50 g (2 oz) celery	2 teaspoons sugar
225 g (8 oz) dried or fresh thin	3 tablespoons rice wine or dry
Chinese egg noodles	sherry
2 tablespoons oil, preferably	300 ml (10 fl oz) vegetable stock
groundnut	2 teaspoons cornflour mixed with
4 garlic cloves, lightly crushed	2 teaspoons water

Finely shred the mushrooms, spring onions and pepper. Coarsely chop the celery.

If you are using dried noodles, cook them according to the instructions on the packet, otherwise boil for 2 minutes until soft. If you are using fresh Chinese noodles, boil for 3 minutes and then drain thoroughly. Scatter the noodles on a baking tray.

Heat a large frying-pan, preferably non-stick, and add 1 tablespoon of the oil. When hot, add the noodles and press down to make the noodles conform to the shape of the pan. Turn the heat to very low, and continue cooking for 10–15 minutes until brown. Flip the noodles over in one piece and continue cooking them until the other side is brown. You may have to add a little oil or water from time to time to keep the noodles moist.

While the noodles are browning, heat a wok or large frying-pan until hot. Add the remaining oil and garlic and stir-fry for a few seconds. Put in the celery, mushrooms and pepper and stir-fry for 3 minutes. Add the mangetout and spring onions and continue to stir-fry for another 2 minutes. Stir in the soy sauces, sugar, rice wine and stock, and bring the mixture to the boil. Thicken with the blended cornflour until the sauce is cooked through.

Take out the noodles and place on a platter. Pour the vegetables and sauce over the noodles and serve at once.

· TAN TAN NOODLES ·

Serves 2

To warm up on a cold afternoon or evening, serve Tan Tan noodles, which I first tasted in a Sichuan restaurant in Hong Kong. Given its Sichuan origin, I expected something spicy – but even so, I was quite unprepared for its explosive quality. The noodles arrived preceded by a wonderful aroma and were served in a bowl shimmering with red chilli oil. It was a delightful experience, featuring the classical spiciness of chilli beans, garlic, ginger and Sichuan preserved vegetable. I immediately tried to recreate the noodles when I returned home. The result is this recipe and I have enjoyed the noodles many times since. An essential ingredient is the Sichuan preserved cabbage or vegetable; it is worth the search and can be found in Chinese grocers. The dish can still be made if you omit it, but the Sichuan preserved cabbage elevates the dish far above the ordinary.

1 tablespoon oil, preferably groundnut
100 g (4 oz) Sichuan preserved cabbage or vegetable, rinsed and finely chopped
1 tablespoon finely chopped garlic
2 teaspoons finely chopped fresh ginger
2 tablespoons rice wine or dry sherry

- *1 tablespoon chilli bean sauce*
- *1 tablespoon Chinese sesame paste or peanut butter*
- *1 tablespoon dark soy sauce*
- *1 tablespoon sugar*
- *450 ml (15 fl oz) vegetable stock*
- *225 g (8 oz) Chinese fresh or dried flat thin wheat or egg noodles*

Heat a wok or large frying-pan over high heat and add the oil. Put in the preserved cabbage or vegetable, garlic and ginger and stir-fry for 1 minute. Add the rice wine, chilli bean sauce, sesame paste, soy sauce, sugar and stock. Reduce the heat and simmer gently for 3 minutes.

Bring a large pan of water to the boil and cook the noodles for 2 minutes if they are fresh and 5 minutes if dried. Drain well in a colander. Divide the noodles into individual bowls and ladle the sauce over them. Serve at once.

· HOT AND SOUR NOODLES ·
Serves 2–4

Hot and sour is a popular combination in Chinese cookery. We Chinese love the two compatible tastes on our palate. This type of noodle dish is often served in snack noodle shops or food stalls in China and Hong Kong. It serves as a fast-food meal that is full of flavour and easily made. I prefer to eat it hot, but it is also good cold.

450 g (1 lb) fresh or dried egg noodles
1 tablespoon sesame oil

Sauce
2 tablespoons dark soy sauce
1 tablespoon chilli oil

1 tablespoon Chinese black rice vinegar or cider vinegar
3 tablespoons finely chopped spring onions
¼ teaspoon freshly ground black pepper
1 teaspoon sugar

If you are using fresh noodles, cook first by boiling them for 3–5 minutes in a large pan of boiling water. If you are using dried noodles, cook in boiling water for 4–5 minutes. Drain the noodles, toss them in the sesame oil and then put aside until required.

Heat all the sauce ingredients in a small pan. Turn the heat down to low and simmer for 5 minutes.

Plunge the noodles into boiling water for 20 seconds, then drain them well in a colander or sieve. Quickly tip the noodles into a large bowl and pour the hot sauce over the top. Mix everything together well and serve at once.

SINGAPORE-STYLE RICE NOODLES

Serves 2–4

Rice noodles are lighter than wheat noodles and therefore lend themselves to dishes that are subtle and delicate. Singapore-style rice noodles are just such a treat. Whenever I visit Singapore or Hong Kong I sample this popular favourite, and I am never disappointed. The thin light noodles blend perfectly with the vegetables and curry sauce. This is equally delicious warm or cold.

225 g (8 oz) rice noodles, rice vermicelli or rice sticks
100 g (4 oz) leeks
100 g (4 oz) carrots
100 g (4 oz) red peppers
4 spring onions
25 g (1 oz) fresh chillies
2 eggs, beaten
2 teaspoons sesame oil
2½ teaspoons salt
2 tablespoons oil, preferably groundnut

Sauce
2 tablespoons curry paste
1 tablespoon finely chopped garlic
1 tablespoon finely chopped fresh ginger
300 ml (10 fl oz) vegetable stock
1 tablespoon sugar
2 tablespoons rice wine or dry sherry
2 tablespoons light soy sauce

Garnish
fresh coriander leaves

Soak the rice noodles in a bowl of warm water for 25 minutes. Drain in a colander. If you are using dried egg noodles, cook for 3–5 minutes in boiling water, drain and immerse them in cold water until required.

Wash and finely shred the white part of the leeks. Finely shred the carrots, peppers, spring onions and chilli. In a small bowl, combine the eggs with the sesame oil and ½ teaspoon of salt.

Heat a wok or large pan over a high heat and add the oil. When almost smoking, add the carrots, leeks, spring onions and remaining salt and stir-fry for a few seconds. Add the peppers and stir-fry for about 1 minute. Put in the curry sauce ingredients and the drained noodles. Stir-fry the mixture for about 5 minutes until well mixed and heated through. Then add the egg mixture, blending thoroughly. Stir-fry for 1 further minute. Serve at once, garnished with fresh coriander.

· CHOW MEIN ·
Serves 4

Chow mein literally means 'stir-fried noodles'. It is a dish of universal popularity based upon its characteristic savoury combination of textures, tastes and colours whether made with meat or, as in this case, with vegetables. Chow mein can be kept warm for at least an hour without losing any of its charm; I enjoy it cold. Serve as an economical family meal or at a buffet party.

225 g (8 oz) fresh or dried egg noodles
50 g (2 oz) celery
50 g (2 oz) tinned bamboo shoots
2 tablespoons oil, preferably groundnut
3 garlic cloves, crushed
1 small onion, finely sliced
175 g (6 oz) small button mushrooms
1 tablespoon light soy sauce

2 tablespoons dark soy sauce
2 teaspoons finely chopped fresh ginger
3 tablespoons vegetable stock
1 tablespoon rice wine or dry sherry
1 teaspoon sugar
100 g (4 oz) bean sprouts

Garnish
fresh coriander sprigs

If you are using fresh noodles, blanch them first in a large pan of boiling water for 3–5 minutes. If you are using the dried noodles, cook in boiling water for 4–5 minutes. Drain the noodles, then put into cold water until required.

String the celery and slice diagonally. Shred the bamboo shoots.

Heat a wok or large frying-pan and add the oil. When moderately hot, add the garlic and stir-fry for 10 seconds. Add the onion, mushrooms, celery and bamboo shoots and stir-fry for about 5 minutes. Drain the noodles thoroughly and put into the wok. Continue to stir-fry for 1 minute, then add the rest of the ingredients, except the bean sprouts. Continue to stir-fry for another 2 minutes, then stir in the bean sprouts. Give the mixture a good stir and turn it onto a serving platter. Garnish with the fresh coriander sprigs.

· LIGHT AND EASY RICE NOODLES ·

Serves 2

Making my way through the streets of Hong Kong and other Asian cities, I have often paused at kerbside food stalls to enjoy this 'fast food' dish. It is light but sustaining and easy to digest as you go about your business. This recipe makes a quick lunch for two using either fresh or dried flat rice noodles.

225 g (8 oz) dried flat rice noodles
or ½ recipe fresh 'fun' rice noodles
(see p.157)

Sauce
2 tablespoons hoisin sauce
1½ tablespoons light soy sauce

2 teaspoons chilli bean sauce
1 tablespoon sesame oil

Garnish
1 tablespoon toasted sesame seeds
(see p.24)

If you are using dried rice noodles, bring a large pan of water to the boil, remove it from the heat and add the rice noodles. Leave to stand for about 10 minutes, then drain thoroughly. If you are using fresh rice noodles, set up a steamer or fill a wok or deep casserole with at least 5 cm (2 in) water. Put a rack into the wok or casserole and bring the water to the boil. Put the rice noodles onto a deep plate and lower the plate into the steamer or onto the rack. Cover the wok tightly. Gently steam on a low heat for 15–20 minutes.

Combine the sauce ingredients and pour over the softened or steamed noodles. Garnish with the sesame seeds and serve.

STIR-FRIED VEGETABLES OVER A RICE NOODLE CLOUD

Serves 4–6

At Chinese banquets when I was a child, the food we children enjoyed most were the dishes that featured fried rice noodles. I believe this is still true today for Western children whose parents take them to Chinese restaurants. Practically any stir-fried dish with a little sauce makes a wonderful topping for these crisp, crackling, crunchy noodles. In this recipe, I combine them with slightly spiced vegetables, enhanced with aromatic seasonings.

300 ml (10 fl oz) oil, preferably groundnut, for deep-frying
175 g (6 oz) rice noodles, rice vermicelli or rice sticks
350 g (12 oz) aubergines
225 g (8 oz) courgettes
3 garlic cloves, crushed
4 spring onions, chopped
2 tablespoons rice wine or dry sherry

- *2 tablespoons yellow bean sauce*
- *2 teaspoons chilli bean sauce*
- *150 ml (5 fl oz) vegetable stock*
- *1 teaspoon sugar*
- *2 tablespoons dark soy sauce*
- *1 teaspoon salt*
- *1 teaspoon cornflour mixed with 1 teaspoon water*

Heat the oil in a deep-fat fryer or large wok until very hot. Deep-fry the noodles until they are crisp and puffed up. Remove with a slotted spoon and drain on kitchen paper. You may have to do this in batches.

Cut the aubergines and courgettes into 7.5 cm (3 in) lengths. Sprinkle them with salt and leave in a sieve to drain for 20 minutes. Rinse under cold running water and pat dry with kitchen paper.

Heat a wok or large frying-pan and add 1½ tablespoons of the oil in which you have fried the noodles. When moderately hot, add the garlic and spring onions and stir-fry for 30 seconds. Add the aubergines and courgettes and continue to stir-fry for 1 minute. Stir in the rest of the ingredients, except for the cornflour mixture, and cook for 3 minutes. Finally add the blended cornflour and cook for a further 1 minute.

Place the deep-fried noodles on a platter and spoon the vegetables over the top. Serve immediately.

· SINGAPORE NOODLES ·
Serves 2

Singapore is a crossroads city in many ways, including the culinary. This delicious noodle recipe reflects just that, with its combination of Indian, Thai and Chinese influences. I enjoyed this dish during my first visit to Singapore, when it became an instant favourite. The noodles used were slightly thicker than the thin fresh egg noodles used here. They contrast perfectly with the fried beancurd cubes, and the finished dish makes a tempting meal for two.

225 g (8 oz) fresh or dried thin egg noodles
225 g (8 oz) firm beancurd
300 ml (10 fl oz) oil, preferably groundnut, for deep-frying
2 teaspoons oil, preferably groundnut
2 eggs, beaten
2 teaspoons sesame oil
½ teaspoon salt
2 tablespoons oil, preferably groundnut

2 garlic cloves, crushed
2 tablespoons light soy sauce
2 teaspoons chilli oil
3 tablespoons tomato purée
2 teaspoons sugar
2 tablespoons finely chopped spring onions
1 fresh chilli, seeded and shredded (optional)

If you are using fresh noodles, blanch them first by boiling for 3–5 minutes in a large pan of boiling water. If you are using dried noodles, cook in boiling water for 4–5 minutes. Drain the noodles, then put into cold water until required. Cut the beancurd into 1 cm (½ in) cubes.

Heat the 300 ml (10 fl oz) of oil in a deep-fat fryer or a large wok until it almost smokes. Deep-fry the beancurd cubes for 1–2 minutes in two batches. When each batch of beancurd cubes is lightly browned, remove and drain well on kitchen paper.

Heat the 2 teaspoons of oil in a wok or frying-pan and add the eggs, sesame oil and salt. When cooked, the eggs should look like a thin, flat pancake. Remove from the pan, roll it up and cut in long 2.5 cm (1 in) wide strips. Set aside.

Heat a wok or large frying-pan and add the 2 tablespoons of oil. When moderately hot, add the garlic and stir-fry for 30 seconds.

Quickly drain the noodles and add them to the pan with the rest of the ingredients. Continue to stir-fry the noodles until all the ingredients are well mixed. Add the egg strips and beancurd and continue to stir-fry for another 3–4 minutes or until the beancurd is heated through.

HOME-MADE CHINESE FRESH 'FUN' RICE NOODLES

Makes about 450 g (1 lb) fresh 'fun' rice noodles

As a young apprentice working in my uncle's restaurant kitchen, I was always fascinated by his skill in making fresh rice noodles. He would make up the batter in the evening and then come in very early the next morning before the restaurant opened to steam the batter into noodles, using five enormous woks. I have never forgotten being impressed by the way he managed to keep all the woks going at once, skipping quickly from one to the other. Freshly made rice noodles are very tasty, with a smooth, soft texture and a velvety surface that combines well with a light coating of sauce, as pasta should.

You should try making your own noodles a few times, if only to see if the freshly made ones really are superior to the packaged version. The rice flour and wheat starch (not the same thing as wheat flour) are readily available at Chinese grocers. The steaming technique assures a moist rice sheet that is easily rolled to be cut into noodles. Be sure to oil the steaming tin each time you add new batter, to prevent sticking. Once rolled and tightly wrapped, the sheets will keep in the fridge for at least 2 days, so you can cut the noodles just before you need to use them. Having mastered the technique and tasted the fresh noodles, I am sure you will make them often. Some Chinese grocers carry ready-made fresh 'fun' noodles.

225 g (8 oz) rice flour
6 tablespoons wheat starch
½ teaspoon salt
300 ml (10 fl oz) water

- *about 2 tablespoons oil, preferably groundnut*
- *1 tablespoon sesame oil*

In a large bowl, combine the rice flour, wheat starch, salt and water. Stir the batter until smooth and strain it through a fine sieve. Stir in the oil and sesame oil. Leave the batter to rest for 30 minutes.

Set up a steamer by adding 5 cm (2 in) water to a wok or deep pan and bring to simmering point. Lightly oil a round baking tin which fits easily into the wok or pan.

Give the batter a good stir and add 5 or 6 tablespoons of the mixture to the baking tin. Gently tip it so that the batter coats the surface of the tin. Place the tin into the wok or pan so that it sits uncovered floating above the simmering water. Cover the wok tightly. Steam gently for 3–4 minutes or until the batter is cooked. Remove the baking tin and allow it to cool slightly. Gently roll up the rice sheet and repeat the process until all the batter is used up.

Cover the rolled up rice sheets with cling film and chill for at least 1 hour before cutting. Cut the sheets into 1 cm (½ in) wide noodles and use immediately. The 'fun' noodles can be steamed and then topped with a sauce or stir-fried.

HOME-MADE CHINESE 'FUN' RICE NOODLES WITH PEPPERS

Serves 4

Occasionally, on hot, humid Chicago summer evenings when my mother was understandably not in the mood for cooking, she would send me out to a local Chinese restaurant for some 'chow fun'. 'Fun' are freshly made soft, tender rice noodles which are usually combined with beef and bitter melon or beef and peppers. Either way, it was delicious. This is my vegetarian version of the dish. The texture of the noodles is a good contrast to that of the colourful, zesty peppers. Once the noodles are made, the rest is a simple stir-fry. Try adding chopped black beans as an experiment.

175 g (6 oz) yellow peppers	1 tablespoon yellow bean sauce
175 g (6 oz) red peppers	2 tablespoons dark soy sauce
100 g (4 oz) green peppers	1 tablespoon rice wine or dry
2 tablespoons oil, preferably	sherry
groundnut	2 tablespoons finely chopped
3 garlic cloves, crushed	spring onions
450 g (1 lb) fresh 'fun' rice noodles	150 ml (5 fl oz) vegetable stock
(see p.157)	1 teaspoon sugar

Cut the peppers into 1 cm (½ in) squares.

Heat a wok or large frying-pan and add the oil. When moderately hot, add the garlic and stir-fry for about 30 seconds. Add the noodles, peppers, yellow bean sauce, soy sauce, rice wine, spring onions, stock and sugar, and stir-fry for about 3 minutes or until the peppers are thoroughly cooked. Turn out on a large serving platter and serve at once.

CHAPTER SEVEN

COLD PASTA
AND
NOODLES

Chinese and Southeast Asian pasta is delicious hot or cold. When you make up the noodle dishes in this chapter, prepare them in basically the same way you would prepare hot noodles. The noodle recipes here are a sampling of my own favourite cold noodle delights. They are ideal for simple buffets and picnics and are more than merely adequate alternatives to hot pasta or noodle dishes.

I include here Spicy Black Bean Sauce Noodles and Cold Sichuan Noodles, which reflect the hot and spicy Chinese style, and Southeast Asian Noodle Salad and Cold Curry-Flavoured Noodles, which deliciously show the creativity of other regional styles. Because cold temperatures affect the potency of spices, it is best to experiment with these recipes to reflect your own personal preference.

COLD CHINESE NOODLE SALAD WITH MUSHROOMS

Serves 2

This is a simple dish that unites two satisfying foods, noodles and mushrooms, in a most appetizing sauce. Hot oils are poured over ginger and spring onions, releasing their tangy flavours; the sauce is allowed to cool, then mixed with the noodles. The mushrooms are cooked separately to preserve their texture.

225 g (8 oz) fresh or dried thin
   Chinese egg noodles
1 tablespoon oil, preferably
   groundnut
2 garlic cloves, crushed
2 tablespoons rice wine or dry
   sherry
1 tablespoon light soy sauce
225 g (8 oz) small button
   mushrooms

Dressing
½ teaspoon freshly ground black
   pepper
3 tablespoons finely chopped
   spring onions
1 tablespoon finely chopped fresh
   ginger
1½ tablespoons light soy sauce
2 tablespoons oil, preferably
   groundnut
1 tablespoon sesame oil

If you are using fresh noodles, blanch first in a large pan of boiling water for 3–5 minutes. Immerse them in cold water. If you are using dried noodles, cook them in boiling water for 4–5 minutes. Drain the noodles, then put them into cold water until required.

Heat a wok or large frying-pan and add the oil. When moderately hot, add the garlic and stir-fry for 30 seconds. Stir in the rice wine, soy sauce and whole button mushrooms and stir-fry for 3 minutes or until the mushrooms are cooked. Remove from the pan and set aside. Wipe the wok clean.

Combine all the dressing ingredients, except the oils, in a small heatproof bowl. Re-heat the wok and add both oils until they begin to smoke. Pour this mixture over the dressing ingredients in the bowl. Drain the noodles thoroughly in a colander. In a large bowl, combine the noodles, mushrooms and dressing. Mix well and serve immediately or within 3 hours.

· CUCUMBER NOODLE SALAD ·
Serves 2

This is a simple vegetarian starter, ideal for warm weather meals. The bean thread noodles have a satiny smooth texture and their light flavour goes well with cucumbers, dressed in a piquant hot and sour sauce.

100 g (4 oz) bean thread (transparent) noodles
225 g (8 oz) cucumbers

Dressing
3 tablespoons light soy sauce
2 tablespoons Chinese white rice vinegar or cider vinegar

- *2 teaspoons chilli oil*
- *1 tablespoon sugar*
- *1 tablespoon oil, preferably groundnut*
- *2 teaspoons finely chopped fresh ginger*
- *3 tablespoons finely chopped spring onions*

Soak the noodles in a large bowl of very hot water for 5 minutes. Drain and immerse them in cold water, then drain thoroughly in a colander. Cut the noodles into 7.5 cm (3 in) lengths, using scissors or a knife.

Peel the cucumbers, slice them in half lengthways and, using a teaspoon, remove the seeds. Cut the cucumber halves into 7.5 cm (3 in) lengths, 5 mm (¼ in) thick.

In a large bowl, combine the dressing ingredients, then add the cucumbers and noodles. Mix thoroughly. Turn the salad onto a serving platter and serve immediately or within 3 hours.

· SOUTHEAST ASIAN NOODLE SALAD ·

Serves 4

On my first visit to Southeast Asia many years ago, what most impressed me was the use of exotic and fascinating combinations of ingredients such as coconut milk, limes, fish sauce and herbs such as basil, all of which were foreign to my tradition. I have since become familiar with these and other once strange ingredients, and my experiments have led me to some very delectable results, as with this light lunch or supper noodle dish, which includes an aromatic combination of splendid tastes and colours.

225 g (8 oz) flat rice noodles
2 spring onions
50 g (2 oz) mangetout
50 g (2 oz) carrots
100 g (4 oz) bean sprouts

Dressing
2 tablespoons fresh lime juice
2 teaspoons chilli oil
2 tablespoons light soy sauce
2 teaspoons sesame oil
1 tablespoon lemon juice
6 tablespoons fresh or tinned coconut milk (see p.14)
½ teaspoon salt

grated rind of 1 lime
½ teaspoon freshly ground black pepper
1 tablespoon sugar
2 tablespoons finely chopped fresh coriander
1½ tablespoons finely chopped fresh ginger
4 tablespoons finely chopped fresh basil

Garnish
3 tablespoons roasted peanuts, coarsely chopped

Bring a large pan of water to the boil, remove from the heat and add the rice noodles. Leave to stand for about 15 minutes, then drain and immerse them in cold water until required.

Finely shred the spring onions, mangetout and carrots. Bring a pan of water to the boil and blanch the bean sprouts, spring onions, mangetout and carrots for 1 minute. Immerse immediately in cold water, drain and set aside.

Combine all the ingredients for the dressing mixture. Drain the noodles thoroughly and toss them with the dressing mixture and the vegetables. Garnish with the peanuts and serve within 3 hours.

COLD CURRY-FLAVOURED NOODLES

Serves 2–4

Cold noodles can take strong flavours because the coldness mutes tastes. Here I have used Southeast Asian spices and seasonings and created a curry sauce strong enough to enliven the cold noodles. The sauce is cooked to bring out its full flavours, then cooled before mixing with the noodles.

450 g (1 lb) dried or fresh Chinese egg noodles

Dressing
1 tablespoon oil, preferably groundnut
2 tablespoons finely chopped garlic
1 tablespoon finely chopped onion
300 ml (10 fl oz) fresh or tinned coconut milk (see p.14)

½ teaspoon turmeric
2 tablespoons curry paste
1 teaspoon salt
1 teaspoon sugar
2 tablespoons light soy sauce

Garnish
fresh basil or fresh coriander leaves

If you are using dried noodles, cook them according to the instructions on the packet or boil for 4–5 minutes. Immerse in cold water until required. If you are using fresh Chinese noodles, boil for 3–5 minutes, then cool them in cold water.

Heat a wok or pan and add the oil. When moderately hot, add the garlic and onion and stir-fry for 2 minutes. Stir in the coconut milk, turmeric, curry paste, salt, sugar and soy sauce and simmer for 4 minutes. Allow the dressing to cool.

Drain the noodles thoroughly and toss with the dressing. Turn onto a platter, garnish with the fresh herbs and serve within 3 hours.

· SESAME BUCKWHEAT NOODLES ·

Serves 2

This simple dish is adapted from a traditional Japanese recipe. The buckwheat noodles have a unique texture that remains excellent when served cold. Perhaps this is because buckwheat, with a different structure from wheat or millet, is not a true cereal. I prefer to use thin buckwheat noodles for their lightness. This recipe will make a satisfying lunch for two.

450 g (1 lb) dried thin Japanese buckwheat 'soba' noodles (see p.157)

Dressing
1 tablespoon chilli oil
2 tablespoons sesame oil
1 tablespoon oil, preferably groundnut
3 tablespoons vegetable stock

2 teaspoons sugar
2 tablespoons light soy sauce
½ teaspoon salt

Garnish
2 tablespoons toasted sesame seeds (see p.24)
2 tablespoons spring onion tops, thinly diagonally sliced

Cook the dried noodles according to the instructions on the packet or boil for 4–5 minutes. Drain, then cool in cold water until required.

Combine the dressing ingredients together in a bowl. Drain the noodles thoroughly and toss them with the dressing. Garnish with the sesame seeds and spring onions and serve.

SPICY CITRUS-FLAVOURED NOODLES

Serves 2–4

This versatile dish is perfect for warm weather eating, picnics, as a starter for an elegant dinner party or for large-scale entertaining. The egg noodles are a natural foil for the zest of the orange and lemon and combine perfectly with the spicy peanut sauce. Mix the noodles with the sauce *only* when you are about to serve the dish. If you prefer the sauce to be even spicier, simply add more chilli oil and garlic.

225 g (8 oz) dried or fresh Chinese egg noodles
1 tablespoon sesame oil

Sauce
1 dried red chilli
grated rind of 1 orange
grated rind of 1 lemon
2 teaspoons oil, preferably groundnut
2 teaspoons sesame paste or peanut butter
2 tablespoons orange juice
2 teaspoons lemon juice
1 teaspoon finely chopped spring onions
1 teaspoon finely chopped garlic
1 tablespoon Chinese white rice vinegar or cider vinegar
1 tablespoon dark soy sauce
2 teaspoons sugar
¼ teaspoon Sichuan peppercorns
2 teaspoons chilli oil

If using dried noodles, cook them according to the packet instructions or boil for 4–5 minutes. Cool in cold water until required. If using fresh noodles, boil for 3–5 minutes, then immerse in cold water. In the same hot water, blanch the dried chilli until soft. Then blanch the lemon and orange rind for 30 seconds to remove their bitterness.

Mix the sauce ingredients together with the chilli in a bowl or in a blender. (This can be done in advance and kept chilled, as the sauce is served cold.)

Drain the cooked noodles, toss them with the sesame oil and arrange on a platter or in a large bowl. Toss the noodles well with the sauce just before serving.

· FRAGRANT RICE NOODLE SALAD ·

Serves 2

This is a refreshing noodle salad from Southeast Asia. Although tomatoes are not indigenous to the region, oriental cooks have been completely won over since their introduction a century ago, and for good reason: they are flavoursome, colourful and nutritious. Except for the Eastern dressing ingredients, this could pass for a zesty Italian pasta dish.

225 g (8 oz) flat rice noodles
225 g (8 oz) tomatoes
50 g (2 oz) Italian (red) onions

Dressing
rind of 1 lime, finely chopped
2 tablespoons lime juice
2 tablespoons light soy sauce
1 tablespoon sugar
1 tablespoon oil, preferably groundnut

- *2 teaspoons finely chopped garlic*
- *1 teaspoon chilli oil*
- *1 teaspoon finely chopped fresh lemon grass*
- *2 tablespoons finely chopped fresh coriander*
- *2 tablespoons finely chopped fresh basil*
- *1 tablespoon finely chopped fresh mint*

Bring a large pan of water to the boil, remove from the heat and add the rice noodles. Leave to stand for about 15 minutes, then drain and immerse in cold water until required.

If you are using fresh tomatoes, skin, seed and coarsely chop. If you are using tinned tomatoes, coarsely chop. Finely slice the onions.

Combine all the dressing ingredients except for the fresh herbs. Thoroughly drain the noodles and toss them with the dressing, herbs, tomatoes and onions. Serve within 3 hours.

• SPICY BLACK BEAN SAUCE NOODLES •

Serves 2

Ever since I can remember, the aroma of black beans cooked with garlic has meant mouth-watering food. Because I enjoy cold noodles, I have adapted these seasonings for a light lunch dish or accompaniment for summer evening meals. The pungent sauce is cooked beforehand and allowed to cool before enlivening the cold noodles.

350 g (12 oz) fresh or dried Chinese egg noodles

Sauce
3 tablespoons oil, preferably groundnut
2 tablespoons yellow bean sauce
2 tablespoons black beans, coarsely chopped
2 tablespoons finely chopped garlic
1 tablespoon finely chopped fresh ginger

- *2 tablespoons finely chopped spring onions*
- *2 teaspoons chilli bean sauce*
- *2 teaspoons sugar*
- *1 tablespoon dark soy sauce*
- *2 teaspoons chilli oil*
- *2 tablespoons rice wine or dry sherry*
- *150 ml (5 fl oz) vegetable stock*
- *1 teaspoon cornflour mixed with 1 teaspoon water*

If you are using fresh noodles, blanch in a large pan of boiling water for 3–5 minutes, then immerse in cold water. If you are using dried noodles, cook in boiling water for 4–5 minutes. Drain the noodles, then put into cold water until required.

For the sauce, heat a wok or large frying-pan and add the oil. When moderately hot, add the yellow bean sauce, black beans, garlic, ginger and spring onions and stir-fry for 2 minutes. Then add the rest of the ingredients, except the cornflour mixture, and continue to cook for 2 minutes. Stir in the blended cornflour and bring to the boil for 30 seconds. Remove from the heat and allow the sauce to cool. Drain the noodles thoroughly in a colander and mix with the sauce. Serve at once.

· COLD SICHUAN NOODLES ·

Serves 2

In this Chinese recipe for spicy noodles, traditionally served hot, I have simply directed that it be eaten cold. This makes a delectable cold salad for warm weather days. It makes an ideal lunch dish for two, but the portions may be increased easily for use in a family meal.

450 g (1 lb) dried or fresh Chinese egg noodles
2 tablespoons oil, preferably groundnut
2 tablespoons finely chopped spring onions
1 tablespoon finely chopped garlic
1 tablespoon yellow bean sauce

2 teaspoons chilli bean sauce
2 teaspoons finely chopped fresh ginger
1 tablespoon rice wine or dry sherry
2 tablespoons dark soy sauce
2 tablespoons sesame oil

Garnish
fresh coriander leaves

If using dried noodles, cook them according to the packet instructions or boil for 4–5 minutes. Cool in cold water until required. If using fresh noodles, boil for 3–5 minutes, then immerse in cold water.

Heat a wok or large frying-pan and add the oil. When hot, add the spring onions, garlic, yellow bean sauce, chilli bean sauce and ginger and stir-fry for 2 minutes. Allow the mixture to cool thoroughly.

Drain the noodles and combine them with the cool seasonings, rice wine, soy sauce and sesame oil. Garnish with coriander and serve within 3 hours.

CHAPTER EIGHT

RICE DISHES

Rice is the staple food of most of the Far East and Asia. Unlike bread, a Western staple that plays only a secondary role in Western cookery, rice is an integral part of every meal and is eaten many times during the day. Left-over rice is stir-fried or dried to use in rice cakes, simmered in a rice porridge, or simply eaten as a snack. Like beancurd, rice combines well with other foods and flavours. Somewhat bland by itself, it readily absorbs other tastes.

Each country treats rice in a different way, ranging from Thai Aromatic Fried Rice to the simple, austere Japanese Rice with Asparagus. Although there are numerous varieties of rice, for everyday use we need only be concerned with three: long-grain, short-grain and glutinous.

LONG-GRAIN RICE

This is the most popular rice for Asian food and is my own favourite, too. Although the Chinese still go through the ritual of washing it, I believe this step can be bypassed with rice purchased at supermarkets. Do not confuse it with the 'easy-cook' and other pre-cooked varieties which are widely available. They are unsuitable for the recipes in this book, except for those using coconut milk, which is rich in fats. It is worth trying to find the Thai aromatic long-grain rice, now available at many Chinese and oriental grocers. It has a pleasing fragrance similar to the basmati rice used in Indian cuisine.

To wash rice

This is an optional step. Put the required amount of rice into a large bowl, fill it with cold water and swish the rice around with your hands. Carefully pour off the cloudy water, keeping the rice in the bowl. Repeat this process several times until the water is clear.

To cook long-grain rice

These basic instructions for long-grain rice are given in my *Illustrated Chinese Cookery* book. The method is easy and foolproof and always produces excellent results.

Fill a glass measuring jug with long-grain rice to the 450 ml (15 fl oz) level.

Put the rice into a large bowl and, if you wish, wash it in several changes of water until the water becomes clear. (This step may be omitted.) Drain the rice and put it into a heavy pan with 900 ml (1½ pints) water and bring to the boil. Continue boiling until most of the surface liquid has evaporated. This should take about 15–20 minutes. The surface of the rice should have small indentations like a pitted crater. At this point, cover the pan with a *very* tight-fitting lid, turn the heat as low as possible and let the rice cook undisturbed for 15–20 minutes. There is no need to 'fluff' the rice before serving it, but it should be thoroughly cooled before stir-frying.

A few rules are worth repeating in regard to long-grain rice:

The water should be at a level 2.5 cm (1 in) above the surface of the rice before boiling; too much water means gummy rice. Recipes on commercial packets generally recommend too much water.

Never uncover the pan once the simmering process has begun; time the process and wait.

SHORT-GRAIN RICE

This rice is not to be confused with pudding rice. Short-grain rice, usually used in Chinese cooking for making porridge, is more popular in Japan. Varieties known as 'American Rose' or 'Japanese Rose' are quite suitable and can be found in many Chinese grocers or in shops that sell Japanese food products. Short-grain is slightly stickier than long-grain white rice, but is cooked in the same way (see opposite) or can be steamed (see p.188).

GLUTINOUS RICE

Glutinous rice is also known as sweet or sticky rice. It is short, round and pearl-like, and is not to be confused with ordinary short-grain or pudding rice. It is sweeter and stickier than ordinary rice when cooked. It is used for substantial rice dishes such as Steamed Sticky Rice, or in stuffings, desserts and for making Chinese rice wine and vinegar. Most Chinese grocers stock it. Glutinous rice must be soaked for at least 2 hours (preferably overnight) before cooking. You may cook it in the same way as long-grain rice (see opposite) or by steaming (see p.188).

· STEAMED STICKY RICE ·

Serves 4

In this recipe, the rice is suffused with many seasonings which are slowly steamed along with it. This is a dish my mother used to cook for me on those days when she could not be home to prepare lunch. She would make the dish and then set it in the warm steamer, where all the ingredients would slowly marry.

glutinous or short-grained rice to fill a measuring jug to 450 ml (15 fl oz) level
100 g (4 oz) fresh or frozen peas
100 g (4 oz) button mushrooms
1 tablespoon oil, preferably groundnut
1 tablespoon finely chopped fresh ginger

3 tablespoons finely chopped spring onions
2 tablespoons finely chopped Sichuan preserved vegetable
3 tablespoons rice wine or dry sherry
1 tablespoon dark soy sauce
2 tablespoons light soy sauce

Put the rice in a large bowl, cover with water and leave to stand for 4 hours or overnight. Drain well. Set up a steamer or put a rack inside a wok or large, deep pan. Pour in about 5 cm (2 in) of water and bring it to the boil. Put the rice in a bowl and place this into the steamer or onto the rack. Cover the pan tightly, turn the heat low and steam gently for about 20 minutes.

If you are using fresh peas, blanch in a pan of boiling water for 3 minutes; drain well. Immerse in cold water to stop them from cooking. Finely slice the mushrooms.

Heat a wok or large frying-pan and add the oil. When moderately hot, add the ginger and spring onions and stir-fry for 2 minutes. Add the mushrooms and Sichuan preserved vegetable and continue to cook for 5 minutes or until most of the liquid has evaporated. Add the rice wine and soy sauces and continue to cook for 2 minutes. Stir in the steamed rice and peas.

Replenish the steamer with hot water. Transfer the rice mixture into a bowl and steam for another 30 minutes over low heat. It is now ready to be served. This rice can be kept warm in the steamer, with the heat turned off, for about half an hour. It also re-heats well.

· THAI AROMATIC FRIED RICE ·

Serves 4

Thai cuisine has been influenced by the Chinese, but there is a great deal of originality in the Thai tradition. This recipe is distinctly Thai in that it uses aromatic sauces, such as chilli bean sauce, soy sauce etc., unlike Chinese fried rice. The soy sauce will leave a rich savoury taste instead of the more pungent taste of Chinese fried rice. The result is an unusually piquant rice dish. Remember the cooked rice should be cooled thoroughly before being stir-fried.

2 tablespoons oil, preferably groundnut
100 g (4 oz) onions, finely chopped
long-grain rice measured to the 450 ml (15 fl oz) level in a measuring jug and cooked (see p.186)
¼ teaspoon salt

- *1 tablespoon light soy sauce*
- *2 teaspoons chilli bean sauce*
- *3 tablespoons tomato purée*
- *3 tablespoons finely chopped spring onions*
- *2 tablespoons finely chopped fresh coriander*
- *4 eggs, beaten*

Heat a wok or large frying-pan and add the oil. When moderately hot, add the onions and stir-fry for 3 minutes. Put in the rice and continue to stir-fry for another 3 minutes. Add the rest of the ingredients, except the eggs. Stir-fry the mixture for a further 5 minutes over a high heat. Next add the beaten eggs and cook for 3 minutes or until the eggs have set. Turn the mixture onto a platter and serve.

SWEETCORN AND GINGER FRIED RICE

Serves 4

Sweetcorn and rice go well together, with their contrasting and complementary textures, colours and flavours. The addition of ginger makes them a little exotic – a true East–West delight. Use fresh corn if possible, and be sure the cooked rice is cold before stir-frying. This will keep it from absorbing too much oil and becoming sticky. This economical and healthy dish may be eaten as a rice salad or vegetable accompaniment to other foods.

450 g (1 lb) fresh sweetcorn on the cob, or 275 g (10 oz) tinned sweetcorn

1 tablespoon oil, preferably groundnut

1½ teaspoons finely chopped fresh ginger

2 tablespoons finely chopped spring onions

2 tablespoons rice wine or dry sherry

long-grain rice measured to the 450 ml (15 fl oz) level in a measuring jug and cooked (see p.186)

¼ teaspoon salt

¼ teaspoon freshly ground pepper

2 tablespoons sesame oil

Remove the corn kernels with a sharp knife or cleaver. You should end up with about 275 g (10 oz). If you are using tinned corn, empty the contents into a sieve, drain well and set aside.

Heat a wok or large frying-pan until hot and add the oil. Put in the ginger and spring onions and stir-fry for a few seconds. Add the rice wine and continue to stir-fry for a few more seconds. Stir in the cold cooked rice and stir-fry for 5 minutes, then add the corn, salt and pepper, and continue to stir-fry for 2 minutes. Finally, add the sesame oil and stir-fry for a further 4 minutes until the corn is thoroughly cooked. Serve at once, or cold as a rice salad.

HONG KONG-STYLE FRIED RICE

Serves 4

One of the many memorable meals I have enjoyed in Hong Kong included a dish of rice, stir-fried with Chinese broccoli stalks and eggs. I first sampled it in the delightful company of the eminent food critic Willie Mark, who guided me to the restaurant that served it. Ordinary broccoli (calabrese) also works well in this recipe.

225 g (8 oz) fresh broccoli or
Chinese broccoli
100 g (4 oz) fresh or frozen peas
2 tablespoons oil, preferably
groundnut
1 teaspoon salt
2 tablespoons water

- long-grain rice measured to the
450 ml (15 fl oz) level in a
measuring jug and cooked
(see p.186)
2 eggs, beaten
2 teaspoons sesame oil

Separate the broccoli heads into florets. Peel the stalks if necessary, then slice. Dice the broccoli into very small pieces.

If you are using fresh peas, blanch in a small pan of boiling water for 2 minutes; if using frozen peas, blanch for 1 minute.

Heat a wok or large frying-pan and add the oil. When moderately hot, add the broccoli, peas and salt and stir-fry for about 1 minute, then add the water. Continue to stir-fry the mixture for about 2 minutes or until the broccoli is cooked. Add the cold cooked rice and stir-fry for 3 minutes. Then add the eggs and sesame oil and stir-fry for a further 2 minutes. Turn the mixture onto a platter and serve at once.

CHINESE RICE PORRIDGE WITH CONDIMENTS

Serves 2

Porridge in the West is a plain yet sustaining dish; in Eastern cookery, porridge is soothing, warm and aromatic. Chinese porridge is usually quite tasty, depending on the flavourings added, and Malaysian porridge is always fiery. This stimulating lunch dish is based upon Malaysian porridge, the seasonings being typical of this cuisine. I like to place the garnish around the porridge before stirring it in because it looks so attractive.

1.2 litres (2 pints) vegetable stock
short-grain rice to fill a
measuring jug to 450 ml
(15 fl oz) level
2 teaspoons salt

Garnish
1 garlic clove
2 spring onions

1 fresh chilli
1 tablespoon finely chopped fresh coriander
1 tablespoon light soy sauce
1 egg
1 teaspoon chilli oil
100 g (4 oz) fresh or tinned tomatoes, chopped
25 g (1 oz) roasted peanuts

Bring the stock to the boil in a large pan and add the rice and salt. Return the mixture to the boil and give it several good stirs. Turn the heat down to low and cover the pan. Simmer for about 45 minutes, stirring occasionally to keep it from sticking.

For the garnish, finely shred the garlic, spring onions and chilli. Arrange the garnishes on a separate platter. When you are ready to serve the porridge, add the garnishes and serve at once.

· PINEAPPLE FRIED RICE ·
Serves 4–6

I first enjoyed this unusual rice dish in Hong Kong and only subsequently learned that it is of Thai origin. Thai cooks commonly hollow out the pineapple and fill it with fried rice or some other tasty stuffing. It is a very attractive way to serve fried rice, but hollowing out the fruit takes a little effort and is not to be done every day. An easier alternative is to cut the pineapple in half lengthways. This is an attractive dish for a special dinner party.

1 large fresh pineapple
25 g (1 oz) Chinese dried mushrooms
2 tablespoons oil, preferably groundnut
1 small onion, finely chopped
100 g (4 oz) Chinese long beans, runner beans or French beans, trimmed and diced

- *long-grain rice measured to the 450 ml (15 fl oz) level in a measuring jug and cooked (see p.186)*
- *2 eggs*
- *2 tablespoons dark soy sauce*
- *1 tablespoon light soy sauce*

Carefully cut off and save the pineapple top, leaving about 2.5 cm (1 in) of the pineapple under the leaves, if you want to use the whole shell for serving. Alternatively, you can cut the pineapple in half lengthways after disposing of the top and leaves. Scoop out the inside fruit, leaving the outer shell of the pineapple intact to serve the fried rice. Coarsely chop the pineapple flesh, discarding the tough centre core.

Soak the dried mushrooms in warm water for 20 minutes until soft. Squeeze out the excess liquid from the mushrooms and remove and discard the stalks. Cut the caps into small dice.

Heat a wok or large frying-pan and add the oil. When almost smoking, add the mushrooms, onion and beans and stir-fry for 1 minute. Mix in the cold cooked rice and stir-fry for 1 minute. Add the eggs and soy sauces and continue to stir-fry for 5 minutes over high heat. Stir in the chopped pineapple and stir-fry for about 2 minutes. Spoon the mixture into the hollowed-out pineapple shell and replace the top, or pile the mixture onto the two halves, and serve the remaining rice on a platter.

· FRAGRANT COCONUT RICE ·

Serves 4

For this recipe you may use 'easy-cook' rice. It is one of those rare dishes in which such pre-cooked rice works well, partly because of the richness and oil in the coconut. Unusual as the combination of spices may seem, you will find them a harmonious blend with this dish. If you use long-grain rice it will be a little sticky, as it should be. The rice re-heats well but should be warmed over a very low heat.

2 tablespoons oil, preferably groundnut
175 g (6 oz) onions, chopped
long-grain or 'easy-cook' rice measured to the 450 ml (15 fl oz) level in a measuring jug
1 teaspoon turmeric
2 teaspoons salt

450 ml (15 fl oz) fresh or tinned coconut milk (see p.14)
150 ml (5 fl oz) vegetable stock
2 whole cloves
1 whole cinnamon stick or Chinese cinnamon bark
2 bay leaves

Heat the oil in a large flameproof casserole until moderately hot. Add the onions and stir-fry for 2 minutes. Put in the rice, turmeric and salt, and continue to cook for 2 minutes.

Add the coconut milk and stock and bring the mixture to the boil. Stir in the whole cloves, cinnamon and bay leaves. Turn the heat as low as possible and cook the rice undisturbed for 20 minutes. It is ready to serve when the rice is cooked.

JAPANESE RICE WITH ASPARAGUS

Serves 2–4

This is a traditional Japanese dish, classic in its simplicity. Appealing to the eye as well as the palate, it is so satisfying that it is almost a meal in itself. This delectable dish is based on short-grain rice. You can substitute broccoli or runner beans for the asparagus.

short-grain rice measured to the 450 ml (15 fl oz) level in a measuring jug
750 ml (1¼ pints) vegetable stock
2 tablespoons light soy sauce
1 tablespoon dark soy sauce
150 ml (5 fl oz) sake, rice wine or dry sherry

450 g (1 lb) fresh asparagus
2 tablespoons oil, preferably groundnut
¼ teaspoon salt
2 tablespoons finely shredded fresh ginger

Cook the rice according to the method given for long-grain rice on p.186, but substitute stock for the water and add the soy sauce and sake.

Cut off the tough ends of the asparagus, then cut the stalks diagonally into 7.5 cm (3 in) long pieces.

Heat a wok or large frying-pan and add the oil. Put in the asparagus pieces and salt and stir-fry for 4 minutes. Remove the asparagus from the pan and leave to cool.

Fold the asparagus and ginger into the warm cooked rice and serve.

· TWO · MUSHROOM RICE ·

Serves 4

This is a simple vegetarian adaptation of a traditional chicken-rice-mushroom dish my mother often made when I was a child. It remains a favourite of mine. One must properly appreciate the mushroom which, in the words of a discriminating scholar, 'belongs to that category of plants used in cooking whose main function is to add less flavour than the spices and herbs, less bulk than the real vegetables, and to absorb differentially the flavours of the dish, in order to bring out, by subtle chemistry, the highest and most delicate tastes'. Once you begin to think of mushrooms in this way and to use them accordingly, all mushroom dishes take on a special charm and flavour. Save the water in which the dried mushrooms have been soaked, as they give an additional earthy flavour to the cooked rice.

25 g (1 oz) Chinese dried mushrooms
900 ml (1½ pints) very hot water
225 g (8 oz) button mushrooms
1 tablespoon oil, preferably groundnut
3 tablespoons finely chopped spring onions

½ teaspoon salt
2 tablespoons light soy sauce
long-grain rice measured to the 450 ml (15 fl oz) level in a measuring jug

Soak the dried mushrooms in the very hot water for 20 minutes until soft. Remove them with a slotted spoon and save the liquid. Squeeze the excess liquid from the mushrooms and remove and discard the stalks. Cut the caps into quarters. Cut the button mushrooms into quarters.

Heat a wok or large frying-pan and add the oil. When hot, add the spring onions, salt and button mushrooms and stir-fry for 2 minutes. Put in the dried mushrooms and stir-fry for another minute or until all the liquid has evaporated. Remove the mixture and set aside.

Add the mushrooms, soy sauce and mushroom liquid to the rice in a pan and bring to the boil. Continue boiling until most of the surface liquid has evaporated. This should take about 15–20 minutes. At this point, cover the pan with a very tight-fitting lid, turn the heat as low as possible and let the rice cook undisturbed with the mushrooms for 15–20 minutes.

Turn onto a platter and serve at once.

. CURRIED FRIED RICE WITH . GREEN BEANS

Serves 4

Curried rice has an appealing and exotic aroma, and beans add colour and a contrast of textures. An exception to the classic rule for stir-frying rice, this cooked rice may be stir-fried immediately, without waiting for it to cool. This is a grand rice dish for any meal.

2 tablespoons oil, preferably groundnut
100 g (4 oz) Chinese long beans, runner beans or French beans, trimmed and diced
long-grain rice measured to the 450 ml (15 fl oz) level in a measuring jug and cooked (see p.186)
1 tablespoons finely chopped garlic

- *3 tablespoons finely chopped fresh coriander*
- *grated rind of ½ lime*
- *2 dried chillies, seeded and chopped*
- *2 tablespoons light soy sauce*
- *2 teaspoons sugar*
- *2 tablespoons curry paste*
- *½ teaspoon salt*

Heat a wok or large frying-pan and add the oil. When moderately hot, add the beans and stir-fry for about 2 minutes. Put in the rice and continue to stir-fry for 3 minutes. Stir in the rest of the ingredients and mix thoroughly. Cook for a further 5 minutes, stirring continuously. Turn the mixture onto a plate and serve at once.

SINGAPORE-STYLE LETTUCE FRIED RICE

Serves 4

This is an easy fried rice dish to make. The chilli adds zest and sparkle to the dish, and the lettuce provides a refreshing touch.

15 g (½ oz) Chinese dried mushrooms

2 tablespoons oil, preferably groundnut

4 shallots, sliced

3 garlic cloves, crushed

long-grain rice measured to the 450 ml (15 fl oz) level in a measuring jug and cooked (see p.186)

50 g (2 oz) fresh or frozen peas

3 tablespoons finely chopped spring onions

2 fresh chillies

2 eggs, beaten

3 tablespoons light soy sauce

½ teaspoon salt

¼ teaspoon freshly ground black pepper

225 g (8 oz) iceberg lettuce, finely shredded

Garnish

2 tablespoons finely chopped spring onions

Soak the dried mushrooms in warm water for 20 minutes until soft. Squeeze the excess liquid from the mushrooms and remove and discard the stalks. Cut the caps into small dice.

Heat a wok or large frying-pan and add the oil. When almost smoking, add the shallots and garlic and stir-fry for 30 seconds. Put in the cold cooked rice and stir-fry for 1 minute, then add the peas, spring onions and chillies and continue to stir-fry for another 3 minutes. Stir in the beaten egg, soy sauce, salt and pepper and stir-fry for a further 2 minutes or until the eggs have set.

Finally, add the lettuce and mix thoroughly. Turn the mixture onto a serving plate and garnish with the spring onions. Serve at once.

CHAPTER NINE

DESSERTS

Chinese, Japanese and Southeast Asian cookery is known throughout the world for its rich variety and savoury tastes rather than for its desserts. Many tend to be oversweet, heavy and rather unappealing to the Western palate. I think fresh fruit in season is generally the best dessert to serve after the subtle richness of this cuisine, but in this short chapter are several more traditional desserts, some based on fruit or delicate egg custard, and including chewy rice balls and sweet crunchy wontons.

COLD HONEYDEW DESSERT SOUP

Serves 6–8

I first sampled this delicious dessert at the Sichuan Garden Restaurant in Hong Kong. It is suffused with the tastes, fragrances, textures and colours popular in Southeast Asia. While in the West we tend to prefer the firm white flesh of mature coconuts, in Southeast Asia the slightly green or immature coconut is preferred. The flesh is quite soft, like a jelly, and can be scooped out with a spoon or one's fingers. The liquid from such coconuts is also rather sweet. Mature coconuts are sweet too, especially when combined with milk and melon. The tapioca adds body to the soup, and the result is an unusually refreshing dessert, perfect after any meal.

4 tablespoons small pearl tapioca
150 ml (5 fl oz) water
1 ripe honeydew melon, about
1.8 kg (4 lb)

750 ml (1¼ pints) fresh or tinned
coconut milk (see p.14)
6 tablespoons sugar

Combine the tapioca and water in a small bowl and leave to stand for 45 minutes.

Cut the honeydew melon into quarters, remove the seeds and cut off the peel. Cut the melon into large pieces. Purée the flesh in a blender to a thick liquid consistency. Pour into a medium-sized bowl and chill.

Place the coconut milk in a pan, add the sugar and tapioca and simmer for 5 minutes or until it thickens. Allow it to cool, then chill.

When you are ready to serve the soup, pour the two separate mixtures into a large serving bowl, stir well and serve.

· SWEET GINGER CUSTARD ·
Serves 10

This creamy smooth and light custard is enlivened by the zest of preserved ginger. This is, in fact, a blend of East and West that works very well. It can be served warm or cold and is a delightful finish to any meal. Make this custard in great quantities because it retains its flavours nicely and one never tires of it. Do not use the Chinese preserved ginger sold in jars with syrup, as it is too strong for this recipe and will overpower the custard.

2 vanilla pods
100 g (4 oz) sugar
600 ml (1 pint) low-fat milk

- *2 tablespoons finely chopped preserved ginger*
- *6 size 1 eggs, beaten*

Split the vanilla pods in half and scrape out the seeds with a spoon. Separate the seeds with 1 tablespoon of the sugar and set to one side.

Pre-heat the oven to 200°C/400°F/Gas 6. Combine the milk, vanilla pods and ginger in a pan and leave it to heat gently. Meanwhile, whisk the eggs, sugar and vanilla seeds in a large bowl. Then, when the milk is steaming hot, discard the vanilla pods and pour the milk into the egg and sugar mixture in a slow and steady stream, whisking until thoroughly blended.

Pour the liquid into a gratin dish and place it in a large roasting tin. Transfer the tin carefully to the oven, then pour in sufficient hot water to come two-thirds up the sides of the dish. Turn the temperature down to 180°C/350°F/Gas 4 and bake for 45 minutes or until done. Serve warm, or cool to room temperature before chilling.

· BANANA CRISPS ·

Serves 4

This is a popular Thai dessert or snack. The bananas must be sliced *very* thinly by hand, not with a food processor. Buy the firmest ones you can find. Indonesians normally use green, underripe bananas, which are easier to slice. Remember that the crisps continue to cook after being removed from the oil, so you must not leave them in for too long. The sugar in the bananas caramelizes as they cool. Your touch with this recipe will improve as you master the method. Once the fried banana slices have cooled thoroughly, they become quite crispy. Serve warm or cold.

3 firm bananas	*groundnut, for deep-frying*
450 ml (15 fl oz) oil, preferably	*caster or icing sugar, for dusting*

Peel and slice the bananas into very thin rounds.

Heat the oil in a deep-fat fryer or wok until hot. Fry several slices of the banana at a time for 2–3 minutes, or until they are a deep golden brown, taking care not to burn them. Drain on kitchen paper and allow to cool. Dust them lightly with sugar and serve.

· CHINESE TOFFEE APPLES ·
Serves 4

There are many versions of this well-known Chinese dessert. I like this one, which I learned in Hong Kong, because it is easy to make. Instead of having to prepare a batter, the apples are simply rolled in cornflour. Some dexterity is required, but that will come with practice, and these apples are so good you will find yourself practising a great deal. I would suggest making it for family consumption a few times before trying it for special guests.

2 medium firm eating apples	▪	*225 g (8 oz) sugar*
juice of 1 lemon	▪	*450 ml (15 fl oz) water*
50 g (2 oz) cornflour	▪	*2 tablespoons white sesame seeds*
450 ml (15 fl oz) oil, preferably	▪	*iced water*
groundnut, for deep-frying	▪	

Peel and core the apples and cut each into 8 large wedges. Mix with the lemon juice to prevent them from browning. Sprinkle the apple wedges with the cornflour until well coated.

Heat the oil in a deep-fat fryer or wok until moderately hot. Lift out several pieces of apple at a time and shake off any excess cornflour. Deep-fry for 2 minutes or until golden. Remove with a slotted spoon and drain on kitchen paper. Repeat the process until you have deep-fried all the apple wedges.

Combine the sugar and water in a pan. Heat the mixture until the sugar melts and begins to caramelize. Turn the heat to *very* low and watch carefully to prevent the syrup from burning. Add the sesame seeds.

Just before serving, prepare a bowl of iced water filled with ice cubes. Re-heat the oil to moderate and deep-fry the apples a second time for about 2 minutes. Drain again on kitchen paper. Gently add the fried apples to the caramel syrup to coat. Remove with a slotted spoon and put the coated apple pieces into the iced water to harden. Do a few at a time to prevent them from sticking together. Remove from the water and place on a serving platter. Serve at once.

· INDONESIAN FRIED BANANAS ·

Serves 2

This naturally sweet and flavoursome dessert is based on an Indonesian recipe but is actually a common treat all over Southeast Asia. It is easy to make and the number of portions may be doubled or trebled.

3 ripe bananas	• 150 ml (5 fl oz) water
50 g (2 oz) plain flour	• 450 ml (15 fl oz) oil, preferably
2 tablespoons sugar	• groundnut, for deep-frying
1 egg, beaten	• caster or icing sugar, for dusting

Peel the bananas and cut them in half widthwise. For the batter, combine the flour, sugar, egg and water in a small bowl. Mix well to form a smooth, thick batter.

Heat the oil in a deep-fat fryer or wok until moderately hot. Put the banana halves into the batter mixture, then lift out the fruit using a slotted spoon and drain off any excess batter. Deep-fry each piece for about 2 minutes until golden and crispy. Remove with a slotted spoon and drain on kitchen paper. Repeat the process until you have fried all the bananas. Arrange them on a serving platter and dust with sugar. Serve at once.

· SWEET WONTONS ·

Makes about 30–35 wontons

In China, these wontons are called firecrackers because of their shape. This recipe is my variation on that popular Chinese theme. Instead of the traditional stuffing of dates, I use sultanas or raisins combined with desiccated coconut and walnuts. The result is a sweet, crunchy and delectable dessert. They may be cooked hours in advance but are tastiest when eaten warm. These wontons are quite addictive; try them just with tea.

1 packet wonton skins (about
30–35 skins)
600 ml (1 pint) oil, preferably
groundnut, for deep-frying
icing sugar for dusting

Filling

- 100 g (4 oz) sultanas or raisins
- 50 g (2 oz) desiccated coconut
- 75 g (3 oz) walnuts, shelled
- 25 g (1 oz) sugar
- grated rind of 1 lemon
- 1 egg, beaten

Combine the filling ingredients together in a large bowl and mix well. Then, using a teaspoon, put a small amount of filling in the corner of each wonton skin. (See drawings below.) Roll it diagonally halfway to the centre, pinch down the sides around the filling, wet the corner with water and fold over to seal well. Gently twist the ends to make an attractive decorative package like a firecracker.

Heat the oil in a deep-fat fryer or large wok until hot. Deep-fry the filled wontons in several batches until they are golden brown, about 3–5 minutes. Remove the cooked wontons with a slotted spoon and drain on kitchen paper. Dust lightly with the icing sugar and serve warm or at room temperature.

MALAYSIAN COCONUT CUSTARD

Serves 6–8

Custards are well known around the world, but coconut custard is specifically Thai and Malaysian in origin. In these countries it is usually steamed, but I find it even better cooked in the traditional Western manner, in a hot water bath in the oven. The rich coconut flavour permeates the custard, making it a perfect dessert served hot or cold. Make it in individual 100 g (4 oz) ramekins if you can.

4 eggs, beaten	***Decoration***
100 g (4 oz) sugar	*100 g (4 oz) desiccated coconut*
450 ml (15 fl oz) fresh or tinned	
coconut milk (see p.14)	
¼ teaspoon salt	

Combine the eggs, sugar, coconut milk and salt in a large bowl and mix well.

Pre-heat the oven to 150°C/300°F/Gas 2.

Pour the custard mixture into individual ramekins or a large baking dish. Place the ramekins or dish inside a large roasting tin. Transfer the tin carefully to the oven, then pour in sufficient hot water to come two-thirds up the sides of the dishes or dish. Bake for 35 minutes if you are using ramekins, or 1 hour if you are using a large baking dish. You can test if the custard is done by inserting the blade of a knife into the centre of the custard. When the custard is done, the blade will come out clean.

Cool and chill the custard until you are ready to serve it. Lightly brown the coconut in a frying-pan over moderate heat. Allow it to cool, sprinkle over the top of the custard and serve.

RICE PUFFS WITH PRUNE FILLING

Makes about 14 rice balls

These sweet rice balls are a satisfying snack or dessert. They were a favourite treat when I was a boy, with their chewy texture and sweet centre. My mother made them with a filling of sweet bean paste, but I find that prunes are just as satisfying. The rice balls will puff up and split slightly as they are heated, but don't worry as they will still retain their shape and centres.

225 g (8 oz) glutinous rice flour	*3 tablespoons white sesame seeds*
300 ml (10 fl oz) hot water	*450 ml (15 fl oz) oil, preferably*
14 prunes, stoned	*groundnut, for deep-frying*

First make the dough. Put the rice flour in a large bowl and gradually stir in the hot water, mixing it all the time with a fork or with chopsticks until most of the water is incorporated. The mixture will be quite sticky. Remove the mixture from the bowl and knead it with your hands until smooth, dusting it with a little rice flour from time to time to keep the dough from sticking. This should take about 5–6 minutes. Put the dough back into the bowl, cover it with a clean, dry tea towel, and leave to rest for about 30 minutes.

If the prunes you are using still have stones in, you can stone them while the dough is resting.

After the resting period, take the dough out of the bowl and knead it again for about 2 minutes, dusting it with a little rice flour if sticky. Once the dough is smooth, form it into a roll about 23 cm (9 in) long and about 2.5 cm (1 in) in diameter. Take a knife and cut the roll into about 14 equal pieces.

Roll each of the dough pieces into a small round pancake about 7.5 cm (3 in) in diameter. Put a prune in the centre of each pancake and bring up the sides pinching the edges to seal well. Roll it into a ball and sprinkle with sesame seeds. Transfer the finished balls to a floured tray and keep them covered until you have filled all the balls in this way.

Heat the oil in a deep-fat fryer or wok until hot. Deep-fry the rice balls in several batches until golden, about 5 minutes. The rice balls will puff up and they may split slightly, popping and splattering fat, so stand well back. Remove with a slotted spoon and drain them on kitchen paper. Serve at once.

▪ SUGGESTED   MENUS ▪

*The following nine menu suggestions are simply a guide to get
you started, as the recipes in this book are very versatile and can
be combined in many different ways for lunches, suppers and
hearty dinners, or for picnics or buffet parties. Use your
imagination to create your own menus, and feel free to mix
oriental dishes with Western food to make the most of both
traditions. Check the number of servings yielded by each
individual recipe and adjust the amounts as required to suit the
number of people you are catering for, taking into account the
number of other dishes you will be providing at the same meal.*

▪ LIGHT LUNCH ▪

BUTTON MUSHROOMS IN SOY SAUCE *(SEE P.114)*
THAI AROMATIC FRIED RICE *(SEE P.189)*
GREEN AND WHITE JADE SALAD *(SEE P.85)*

Vegetables are a perfect solution for a light lunch. The mushrooms
in a savoury sauce are served with a very aromatic and satisfying Thai-
flavoured fried rice dish and a simple salad. Fresh fruit is always the
best solution for a light lunch dessert. The mushroom dish can be
made in advance and re-heats well. (See photograph on pages 66–67.)

▪ FAMILY MEAL ▪

TANGY TOMATO SOUP WITH LEMON GRASS *(SEE P.61)*
CHOW MEIN *(SEE P.168)*
CRISPY VEGETABLE STIR-FRY *(SEE P.131)*
MALAYSIAN COCONUT CUSTARD *(SEE P.206)*

This inspired menu could easily persuade your family to adopt the vegetarian style every day. The soup is a zesty and refreshing opener. Chow mein, of course, has a universal appeal and is a welcome addition to any meal. It is accompanied by the crunchy textured vegetable stir-fry, and finally there is a flavoured custard that is sure to please everyone. It can be served hot or cold. (See photograph on pages 68–69.)

▪ DINNER PARTY ▪

ASPARAGUS WITH TANGY MUSTARD DRESSING *(SEE P.90)*
BRAISED CHINESE MUSHROOMS *(SEE P.129)*
FRAGRANT COCONUT RICE *(SEE P.194)*
BEAN SPROUT SALAD *(SEE P.89)*
SWEET GINGER CUSTARD *(SEE P.201)*

Dinner parties offer one of the best reasons to cook for friends. Begin your meal with the asparagus, an elegant starter that sets the tone for the entire dinner. Braised Chinese Mushrooms can be made ahead of time and re-heats well – it is a dish often served at Chinese banquets. The coconut rice is a flavoursome departure from the usual. A refreshing note is provided by the salad, which prepares you for the dessert. Sweet Ginger Custard is an Eastern variation of the universally popular vanilla custard, and rounds off the meal nicely. (See photograph on pages 70–71.)

· PARTY BUFFET ·

SUGAR WALNUTS *(SEE P.43)*
CRISPY WONTONS *(SEE P.52)*
JAPANESE-STYLE MARINATED MUSHROOMS *(SEE P.55)*
SPICY CITRUS-FLAVOURED NOODLES *(SEE P.181)*
MOCK VEGETABLE PASTA *(SEE P.104)*
PINEAPPLE FRIED RICE *(SEE P.193)*
EAST–WEST SHREDDED SALAD *(SEE P.86)*

This is a delightful menu sure to please even non-vegetarians. Much of the work can be done beforehand. The Sugar Walnuts can be made up to two days in advance. Both the mushroom and noodle dishes can be made the night before. The Mock Vegetable Pasta can be made the morning of the buffet and will keep for hours in the fridge. Although the Pineapple Fried Rice is usually eaten hot, I find the sweet tartness of the pineapple equally appealing at room temperature. The salad is simple to make, and once the ingredients are prepared it takes but minutes to put it together. The wontons should ideally be fried just before serving. I would serve fresh fruit as the most appropriate dessert. (See photograph on pages 106–107.)

· COSY AUTUMN SUPPER ·

SESAME-DRESSED SPINACH SALAD *(SEE P.84)*
SAVOURY BEANCURD CASSEROLE *(SEE P.139)*
LONG-GRAIN RICE *(SEE P.186)*
SWEET WONTONS *(SEE P.204)*

This simple but savoury menu is perfect for cool autumn evenings. It begins with a sparkling spinach salad which can be made in the morning. The substantial and savoury beancurd dish may also be prepared in advance: it re-heats well and is perfect over steamed long-grain rice. After all these nutritious foods, I like to indulge in crispy Sweet Wontons, which can also be made ahead of time. Serve them with Western vanilla ice cream – the best of East and West! (See photograph on pages 108–109.)

· COLD WINTER FEAST ·

FIERY SICHUAN SOUP *(SEE P.77)*
CURRIED FRIED RICE WITH GREEN BEANS *(SEE P. 197)*
VIETNAMESE-STYLE VEGETABLES *(SEE P.132)*
INDONESIAN FRIED BANANAS *(SEE P.204)*

Cold winter evenings make for hearty appetites. This is a feast for family and friends, and the portions can easily be doubled. It begins with a hot and sour version of a well-known Chinese soup that is sure to warm body and soul. I would follow this with a warming rice dish with crunchy green beans and the substantial Vietnamese-style vegetables. The fried bananas make a tempting finishing touch, one that goes well with a good port. (See photograph on pages 110–111.)

· ORIENTAL-STYLE PICNIC ·

COLD SICHUAN NOODLES *(SEE P.184)*
CRUNCHY RADISH SALAD *(SEE P.56)*
STIR-FRIED SPICY CARROTS *(SEE P.127)*
COLD HONEYDEW DESSERT SOUP *(SEE P.200)*

Picnics are a great favourite of mine, and foods flavoured with oriental spices add an exotic touch. This picnic menu is easy to assemble as the dishes can be made the day or night before and allowed to cool thoroughly, before being properly wrapped for the next day. Although the spicy carrots are usually served hot, I find them equally delicious cold. The salad offers a calming contrast to the noodles and carrots, both of which contain strong spices. The cold sweet soup has just the right cooling touch and makes a grand finale to the picnic. (See photograph on pages 146–147.)

· COCKTAIL PARTY ·

HOT AND SPICY WALNUTS *(SEE P.45)*
CRISPY BEANCURD CUBES WITH PEANUT DIPPING SAUCE *(SEE P.144)*
WINTER VEGETABLE FRITTERS *(SEE P.51)*
GRILLED MUSHROOMS WITH LEMON SAUCE *(SEE P.125)*
VEGETABLE MEDLEY WITH TOMATO-GARLIC SAUCE *(SEE P.116)*

Cocktail parties are especially fun when good food is served. The food must be manageable so your guests can easily pick it up with cocktail sticks or fingers. And it must be easy on the host or hostess, so time can be spent with the guests. Therefore, most of this menu can be prepared hours in advance and all of it is 'finger-food'. The walnuts can be made the day before and re-crisped in the oven before serving. The dipping sauce can be made the night before, but the beancurd should be fried at the last possible moment. The fritters can be prepared at least 1 hour in advance and kept warm in a low oven. The grilled mushrooms are served at room temperature with the sauce made well in advance. Use the colourful vegetable medley as the centrepiece of your party, and prepare it the night before if necessary. (See photograph on pages 148–149.)

· DINNER IN A HURRY FOR TWO OR MORE ·

SPINACH AND EGG-RIBBON SOUP *(SEE P.75)*
SESAME BUCKWHEAT NOODLES *(SEE P.180)*
STIR-FRIED LETTUCE *(SEE P.121)*

This is a quick, nutritious dinner for two or more: the portions can easily be increased. The soup is a light stock with spinach and egg ribbons. The buckwheat noodles are satisfying and can be served warm or cold. They can be made ahead of time and kept in the fridge, but bring them to room temperature before serving. The lettuce takes but minutes to prepare and stir-fry. Fresh fruit is a sensible and delicious way to finish off this speedy yet wholesome meal. (See photograph on pages 150–151.)

· I N D E X ·